NO FEAR SHAKESPEARE

NO FEAR SHAKESPEARE

Antony and Cleopatra

As You Like It

The Comedy of Errors

Hamlet

Henry IV, Parts One and Two

Henry V

Julius Caesar

King Lear

Macbeth

The Merchant of Venice

A Midsummer Night's Dream

Much Ado About Nothing

Othello

Richard III

Romeo and Juliet

Sonnets

The Taming of the Shrew

NO FEAR SHAKESPEARE

ANTONY AND CLEOPATRA

SPARK NOTES

SPARKNOTES is a registered trademark of SparkNotes LLC

Spark Publishing
120 Fifth Avenue
New York, NY 10011
www.sparknotes.com

Please submit all comments and questions or report errors to www.sparknotes.com/errors.

ISBN-13: 978-1-4114-9919-5
ISBN-10: 1-4114-9919-0

Library of Congress Cataloging-in-Publication Data

Shakespeare, William, 1564–1616.
    Antony and Cleopatra.
        p. cm. — (No fear Shakespeare)
    Summary: Presents the original text of Shakespeare's play side by side with a modern version, with marginal notes and explanations and full descriptions of each character.
    1. Antonius, Marcus, 83?–30 B.C.—Drama. 2. Cleopatra, Queen of Egypt, d. 30 B.C.—Drama. 3. Rome—History—Civil War, 43–31 B.C.—Drama. 4. Egypt—History—332–30 B.C.—Drama. 5. Romans—Egypt—Drama. I. Title. II. Series: Shakespeare, William, 1564–1616. No fear Shakespeare.

PR2802.A1 2006
822.3'3—dc22

                                           2006015029

Printed and bound in the United States of America

20 19 18 17 16

There's matter in these sighs, these profound heaves.
You must translate: 'tis fit we understand them.

(*Hamlet*, 4.1.1–2)

FEAR NOT.

Have you ever found yourself looking at a Shakespeare play, then down at the footnotes, then back at the play, and still not understanding? You know what the individual words mean, but they don't add up. SparkNotes' *No Fear Shakespeare* will help you break through all that. Put the pieces together with our easy-to-read translations. Soon you'll be reading Shakespeare's own words fearlessly—and actually enjoying it.

No Fear Shakespeare puts Shakespeare's language side-by-side with a facing-page translation into modern English— the kind of English people actually speak today. When Shakespeare's words make your head spin, our translation will help you sort out what's happening, who's saying what, and why.

ANTONY AND CLEOPATRA

ACT FOUR

ACT FIVE

CHARACTERS

Mark Antony—One of three members of the triumvirate that jointly rules the Roman Empire, the other members being Octavius Caesar and Lepidus. Antony was once a feared and respected soldier, but his credibility and authority have diminished due to his high-profile love affair with Cleopatra. As the play opens, Antony has retreated to Egypt to be close to Cleopatra. He soon finds himself torn between the Western world of duty and reason—represented by Rome—and the Eastern world of desire and pleasure—reflected in Egypt and his love for Cleopatra. Antony feels the need to reaffirm the honor that has made him a celebrated Roman hero, but he cannot deny the love that continually draws him to Cleopatra.

Cleopatra—The queen of Egypt and Antony's lover. A powerful and attractive woman, Cleopatra derives much joy from the emotional and physical control she wields over Antony. Her emotions are as volatile as they are theatrical, which is seen in her explosive and sensual attempts to manipulate Antony. While her actions and emotions often seem artificial and self-consciously dramatic, her love for Antony appears genuine.

Octavius Caesar—The second member of the triumvirate that rules the Roman Empire. Octavius is the nephew and adopted son of Julius Caesar. Ambitious and extremely pragmatic, Octavius lacks Antony's military ability as a general, but his stoic reasoning and political savvy guarantee his success and prevent him from succumbing to the heroic or romantic folly that plagues Antony. Throughout the play, Octavius is placed in opposition to Cleopatra as representations of West and East, respectively.

Lepidus—The third member of the triumvirate that rules the Roman Empire. Marcus Aemilius Lepidus lacks the political and personal strength of Octavius and Antony. Lepidus attempts to keep peace between Octavius and Antony but ultimately fails and is later imprisoned by Octavius for treason.

Sextus Pompeius (Pompey)—The son of a great general. Pompey's youth and popularity are matched by his military strength and expertise. He is a legitimate threat to the triumvirate, but his honor prevents him from taking advantage of political opportunities that arise. He refuses to let his men to kill the unsuspecting Caesar, Antony, and Lepidus when they are his guests.

Domitius Enobarbus—Antony's lieutenant and most loyal supporter. Enobarbus is wise and often sarcastic. He is devoted to Antony, despite Antony's political and military blunders. Enobarbus eventually leaves his master to serve Octavius, but soon laments his choice, realizing that, for him, loyalty is above all.

Octavia—Octavius Caesar's sister. Octavia marries Antony in order to cement an alliance between the two triumvirs. She is the paradigm of Roman womanhood and a dutiful wife, but this also makes her vulnerable to Antony's deception.

Charmian and **Iras**—Cleopatra's faithful attendants.

The Soothsayer—An Egyptian fortuneteller who foresees that Antony's fortune will always pale in comparison to Caesar's.

Dolabella—One of Octavius Caesar's men. Dolabella guards the captive Cleopatra.

Agrippa—One of Octavius Caesar's officers. Agrippa is a confidant of Octavius and a leader of Octavius's army. Agrippa leads the retreat from Antony's unexpectedly powerful forces.

Camidius—A general in Antony's army. Camidius surrenders and defects to Caesar's side after the battle in which Antony follows Cleopatra's lead and flees.

Ventidius—A Roman soldier under Antony's command. Ventidius leads the legions to victory against the kingdom of Parthia. Though an effective solider, he is cautious in battle for fear that winning too much glory would sour his relationship with Antony.

Scarus—A courageous and faithful soldier serving under Antony. He garners fantastic wounds in the battle against Caesar's army. Throughout the play, Scarus remains loyal to Antony.

Proculeius—One of Caesar's soldiers, who proves untrustworthy.

Diomedes—A servant of Cleopatra. Diomedes is sent to deliver a message to Antony that Cleopatra has not committed suicide.

Eros—An attendant serving Antony. To avoid taking his own life, Antony commands Eros to kill him; however, Eros's love for Antony prevents him from complying with Antony's wishes.

Menas—An ambitious young soldier under Pompey. During the dinner party that Pompey hosts for the triumvirate, Menas asks for permission to kill Caesar, Antony, and Lepidus, which would result in the control of the world falling into his master's hands.

Seleucus—Cleopatra's treasurer, who betrays her.

Countryman—An Egyptian who brings a basket of figs containing poisonous snakes to Cleopatra.

Decretus—One of Antony's soldiers.

ANTONY AND CLEOPATRA

ACT ONE

SCENE 1

Enter DEMETRIUS *and* PHILO

PHILO

Nay, but this dotage of our general's
O'erflows the measure. Those his goodly eyes,
That o'er the files and musters of the war
Have glowed like plated Mars, now bend, now turn
5　The office and devotion of their view
Upon a tawny front. His captain's heart,
Which in the scuffles of great fights hath burst
The buckles on his breast, reneges all temper
And is become the bellows and the fan
10　To cool a gypsy's lust.

Flourish. Enter ANTONY, CLEOPATRA, *her ladies, the train,
with eunuchs fanning her*

　　　　　　　　Look where they come.
Take but good note, and you shall see in him
The triple pillar of the world transformed
Into a strumpet's fool. Behold and see.

CLEOPATRA

If it be love indeed, tell me how much.

ANTONY

15　There's beggary in the love that can be reckoned.

CLEOPATRA

I'll set a bourn how far to be beloved.

ANTONY

Then must thou needs find out new heaven, new earth.

ACT ONE

SCENE 1

DEMETRIUS *and* PHILO *enter.*

PHILO

No, our general's infatuation is out of control. His eyes used to glow with pride when he reviewed his troops. Now his eyes devote themselves exclusively to a certain brown-skinned face. His heart used to burst the buckles on his breastplate in great fights, but now he's lost all temperance and dedicates his heart to satisfying the lust of an Egyptian whore.

Important people had their own signature trumpet flourish that announced their entrances to and exits from a room or space. Trumpeters were part of their entourage.

A trumpet fanfare announces the entrance of ANTONY, CLEOPATRA, *her ladies and attendants, and eunuchs with fans.*

Look at them. Take a good look, and you'll see that one of the three men who rule the world has turned into a whore's jester. Look and see.

CLEOPATRA

If what you feel is really love, tell me how much.

ANTONY

It would be a pretty stingy love if it could be counted and calculated.

CLEOPATRA

I want to measure the extent of your love, to see how far it stretches.

ANTONY

Then you would have to go beyond heaven, beyond earth.

Enter a MESSENGER

MESSENGER
News, my good lord, from Rome.

ANTONY
Grates me, the sum.

CLEOPATRA
20 Nay, hear them, Antony.
Fulvia perchance is angry. Or who knows
If the scarce-bearded Caesar have not sent
His powerful mandate to you, "Do this, or this.
Take in that kingdom, and enfranchise that.
25 Perform 't, or else we damn thee."

ANTONY
                                        How, my love?

CLEOPATRA
Perchance? Nay, and most like.
You must not stay here longer. Your dismission
Is come from Caesar. Therefore hear it, Antony.
Where's Fulvia's process? Caesar's, I would say—both?
30 Call in the messengers. As I am Egypt's queen,
Thou blushest, Antony, and that blood of thine
Is Caesar's homager. Else so thy cheek pays shame
When shrill-tongued Fulvia scolds. The messengers!

ANTONY
Let Rome in Tiber melt and the wide arch
35 Of the ranged empire fall. Here is my space.
Kingdoms are clay. Our dungy earth alike
Feeds beast as man. The nobleness of life
Is to do thus, when such a mutual pair
And such a twain can do 't, in which I bind,
40 On pain of punishment, the world to weet
We stand up peerless.

A MESSENGER *enters.*

MESSENGER

I have news from Rome, my good lord.

ANTONY

Which irritaties me. Give me a summary.

CLEOPATRA

Fulvia is Marc
Antony's wife.

Octavius Caesar
was only in his
twenties at this
time, about
twenty years
younger than
Antony.

No, listen to it, Antony. Perhaps Fulvia is angry with you. Who knows, maybe the baby-faced Caesar has orders for you: "Do this, do that; conquer that kingdom, liberate this one. Do it or we'll condemn you."

ANTONY

What, my love?

CLEOPATRA

Maybe? No, most likely. You can't stay here any longer. Caesar has sent your dismissal, so pay attention, Antony. Where's Fulvia's summons—excuse me, I should have said Caesar's. Or do Fulvia and Caesar both beckon you back to Rome? Call in the messengers and we'll find out. As surely as I am the queen of Egypt, Antony, you're blushing, which means you're Caesar's servant. Or that that bitch Fulvia still has the power to humiliate you. Call the messengers!

ANTONY

Rome was built
on the river
Tiber.

Let Rome be washed away in the Tiber and let the great empire fall. My place is here. Kingdoms are only dirt. The soil feeds animals as well as people, so how does having a kingdom separate humans from beasts? The noblest thing is to do what we're doing, particularly when the couple is as well matched as we are. I demand that the world admit we are the perfect couple or else suffer the consequences.

CLEOPATRA
Excellent falsehood!
Why did he marry Fulvia, and not love her?
I'll seem the fool I am not. Antony
Will be himself.

ANTONY
But stirred by Cleopatra.
45 Now, for the love of Love and her soft hours,
Let's not confound the time with conference harsh.
There's not a minute of our lives should stretch
Without some pleasure now. What sport tonight?

CLEOPATRA
Hear the ambassadors.

ANTONY
Fie, wrangling Queen!
50 Whom every thing becomes—to chide, to laugh,
To weep, whose every passion fully strives
To make itself, in thee, fair and admired!
No messenger but thine, and all alone
Tonight we'll wander through the streets and note
55 The qualities of people. Come, my Queen,
Last night you did desire it.—*(to the* **MESSENGER***)* Speak not
to us.
Exeunt **ANTONY** *and* **CLEOPATRA** *with the train*

DEMETRIUS
Is Caesar with Antonius prized so slight?

PHILO
Sir, sometimes when he is not Antony
He comes too short of that great property
60 Which still should go with Antony.

DEMETRIUS
I am full sorry
That he approves the common liar, who
Thus speaks of him at Rome, but I will hope
Of better deeds tomorrow. Rest you happy!
Exeunt

CLEOPATRA

(to herself) What an enormous lie! Why did he marry Fulvia if he didn't love her? I'll pretend to be a fool and believe him. He'll never change.

ANTONY

(overhearing the last sentence) Unless he is moved and inspired by Cleopatra. Now, since we love the feeling of being in love, let's not spoil the mood with serious discussion. We shouldn't spend a minute without some kind of amusement. What shall we do tonight?

CLEOPATRA

Meet with the ambassadors.

ANTONY

Shame on you, stubborn Queen! Everything you do is attractive—scolding, laughing, crying—every emotion seems admirable when you express it. I won't see any messengers but yours. Tonight we'll wander through the streets and observe the people. Come, my Queen. That's what you wanted to do last night. (to the MESSENGER) Don't talk to us.

ANTONY and CLEOPATRA exit with their attendants.

DEMETRIUS

Does Antony have so little respect for Caesar?

PHILO

Sir, sometimes he's like a different person, a person who can't measure up to the former Antony.

DEMETRIUS

I'm sad to say this confirms the stories being told about him in Rome, which I had taken to be lies. Well, I'll hope things change for the better soon. Have a good night!

They exit.

ACT 1, SCENE 2

Enter ENOBARBUS, LAMPRIUS, *a* SOOTHSAYER, *Rannius,*
LUCILLIUS, CHARMIAN, IRAS, MARDIAN *the eunuch, and*
ALEXAS

CHARMIAN
Lord Alexas, sweet Alexas, most anything Alexas, almost
most absolute Alexas, where's the soothsayer that you
praised so to th' Queen? Oh that I knew this husband,
which, you say, must charge his horns with garlands!

5 ALEXAS
Soothsayer!

SOOTHSAYER
Your will?

CHARMIAN
(to ALEXAS*)* Is this the man? *(to* SOOTHSAYER*)* Is 't you, sir,
that know things?

SOOTHSAYER
In nature's infinite book of secrecy
A little I can read.

ALEXAS
(to CHARMIAN*)*   Show him your hand.

10 ENOBARBUS
(to servants within) Bring in the banquet quickly. Wine
                enough
Cleopatra's health to drink.

CHARMIAN
(giving hand to SOOTHSAYER*)* Good sir, give me good
                fortune.

SOOTHSAYER
I make not, but foresee.

ACT 1, SCENE 2

ENOBARBUS, LAMPRIUS, *the* FORTUNETELLER, *Rannius,* LUCILLUS, CHARMIAN, IRAS, MARDIAN *the eunuch, and* ALEXAS *enter.*

CHARMIAN

Lord Alexas, sweet Alexas, most anything Alexas, almost the most consummate Alexas, where's the fortuneteller you recommended so highly to the Queen? Oh, I only wish I knew the name of that husband you said he predicted will have a cheating wife!

ALEXAS

(calling) Fortuneteller!

FORTUNETELLER

What can I do for you?

CHARMIAN

(to ALEXAS*)* Is this the man you recommended? *(to the* FORTUNETELLER*)* Are you the man who knows the future?

FORTUNETELLER

I can understand a few of nature's infinite secrets.

ALEXAS

(to CHARMIAN*)* Give him your hand to read.

ENOBARBUS

(to the servants) Bring the dessert in right away, and make sure there's enough wine to toast Cleopatra's health.

CHARMIAN

(giving her hand to the FORTUNETELLER*)* Kind sir, give me a good fortune.

FORTUNETELLER

I don't make fortunes; I only see them.

CHARMIAN
Pray, then, foresee me one.

SOOTHSAYER
15   You shall be yet far fairer than you are.

CHARMIAN
(to the others) He means in flesh.

IRAS
No, you shall paint when you are old.

CHARMIAN
Wrinkles forbid!

ALEXAS
Vex not his prescience. Be attentive.

CHARMIAN
20   Hush!

SOOTHSAYER
You shall be more beloving than beloved.

CHARMIAN
I had rather heat my liver with drinking.

ALEXAS
Nay, hear him.

CHARMIAN
Good now, some excellent fortune! Let me be married to
25   three kings in a forenoon and widow them all. Let me have
a child at fifty, to whom Herod of Jewry may do homage.
Find me to marry me with Octavius Caesar, and companion
me with my mistress.

CHARMIAN

Then see a good one for me.

FORTUNETELLER

Your beauty will be even greater than it is now.

CHARMIAN

(to the others) He means I'll get fat.

IRAS

No, he means you'll use makeup when you're old.

CHARMIAN

May my wrinkles forbid that!

ALEXAS

Don't joke about his predictions. Pay attention.

CHARMIAN

Quiet!

FORTUNETELLER

You will love more than you are loved.

CHARMIAN

I would rather get passion from drink than from love.

Passion was thought to originate in the liver, which could be stimulated by drink.

ALEXAS

Just listen to him.

CHARMIAN

Be kind now and tell me some excellent fortune. Tell me that I'll marry three kings before noon and be widowed by all of them. Tell me I'll have a child when I'm fifty who will be honored even by Herod of Judea. Let me marry Octavius Caesar and become my Queen's equal.

Herod was the Roman governor of Israel at the time of Christ's birth. In an attempt to kill Jesus, prophesied to become king of the Jews, Herod ordered the slaughter of all the infants in Bethlehem.

SOOTHSAYER
You shall outlive the lady whom you serve.

CHARMIAN
30 Oh, excellent! I love long life better than figs.

SOOTHSAYER
You have seen and proved a fairer former fortune
Than that which is to approach.

CHARMIAN
Then belike my children shall have no names. Prithee, how
many boys and wenches must I have?

SOOTHSAYER
35 If every of your wishes had a womb,
And fertile every wish, a million.

CHARMIAN
Out, fool! I forgive thee for a witch.

ALEXAS
You think none but your sheets are privy to your wishes.

CHARMIAN
(to SOOTHSAYER*)* Nay, come, tell Iras hers.

ALEXAS
40 We'll know all our fortunes.

ENOBARBUS
Mine, and most of our fortunes tonight, shall be—drunk to
bed.

IRAS
(giving her hand to the SOOTHSAYER*)* There's a palm
presages chastity, if nothing else.

CHARMIAN
45 E'en as the o'erflowing Nilus presageth famine.

FORTUNETELLER

You will outlive the Queen.

CHARMIAN

Figs were thought to resemble female genitalia.

Oh, excellent! I love long life better than figs.

FORTUNETELLER

You have already had better fortune than the future will bring.

CHARMIAN

Then my children will probably be illegitimate. Tell me, please: how many boys and girls will I have?

FORTUNETELLER

If every time you wished for a child you could have had one, you would have a million children.

CHARMIAN

Get out of here, you fool! Since you're a fortuneteller I won't bring charges of witchcraft against you.

ALEXAS

You seem to think no one outside of your bedroom knows what you wish.

CHARMIAN

(*to* **FORTUNETELLER**) Never mind. Tell Iras's fortune.

ALEXAS

We'll all want our fortune told.

ENOBARBUS

My fortune—like that of many of us tonight—is to go drunk to bed.

IRAS

(*giving her hand to the* **FORTUNETELLER**) There's a palm that will predict a chaste life, if nothing else.

CHARMIAN

The Nile River overflowed its banks every year, irrigating the surrounding farmland and guaranteeing a good harvest.

Like the overflowing Nile predicts famine.

IRAS
Go, you wild bedfellow, you cannot soothsay.

CHARMIAN
Nay, if an oily palm be not a fruitful prognostication, I cannot scratch mine ear.—Prithee, tell her but a workaday fortune.

SOOTHSAYER
50 Your fortunes are alike.

IRAS
But how, but how? Give me particulars.

SOOTHSAYER
I have said.

IRAS
Am I not an inch of fortune better than she?

CHARMIAN
Well, if you were but an inch of fortune better than I, where
55 would you choose it?

IRAS
Not in my husband's nose.

CHARMIAN
Our worser thoughts heavens mend. Alexas! *(to* **SOOTHSAYER***)* Come, his fortune, his fortune! Oh, let him marry a woman that cannot go, sweet Isis, I beseech thee,
60 and let her die too, and give him a worse, and let worse follow worse, till the worst of all follow him laughing to his grave, fifty-fold a cuckold! Good Isis, hear me this prayer, though thou deny me a matter of more weight, good Isis, I beseech thee!

IRAS
65 Amen, dear goddess, hear that prayer of the people! For, as it is a heartbreaking to see a handsome man loose-wived, so it is a deadly sorrow to behold a foul knave uncuckolded.

IRAS

Oh stop it, you lusty bed-hopper. You can't see the future.

CHARMIAN

Well, if a moist palm isn't a clear sign of promiscuity, then I can't scratch my own ear. *(to* FORTUNETELLER*)* Please, tell her an ordinary fortune.

FORTUNETELLER

Your fortunes are the same.

IRAS

But how? How is that possible? Give me details.

FORTUNETELLER

I've said what I have to say.

IRAS

Isn't my fortune just a little better than hers? By an inch, even?

CHARMIAN

Well, if you could have just an inch of better fortune than me, where would you like the improvement?

IRAS

Not in my husband's nose.

CHARMIAN

May heaven save us from indecent thoughts! Alexas! *(to the* FORTUNETELLER*)* Come and tell his fortune. Let him marry a woman he can't satisfy, dear Isis, I pray! And then let her die, and give him someone worse. Then let *her* die, and let her replacement be even worse. And so on until the last one, who is unfaithful with at least fifty other men and laughs at him until he dies. I beg you to grant my prayer, good Isis, even though it means you deny me something more important for myself. Good Isis, I beg you!

Isis was Egypt's primary female deity, generally associated with the earth, the moon, and fertility.

IRAS

Amen, dear goddess. Listen to our prayer. If it's sad to see a handsome man with a cheating wife, it's a tragedy to see an ugly thug with a wife who's faithful.

Therefore, dear Isis, keep decorum, and fortune him
accordingly.

CHARMIAN
70   Amen.

ALEXAS
          (to himself) Lo now, if it lay in their hands to make me a
          cuckold, they would make themselves whores but they'd do 't.

ENOBARBUS
          Hush! Here comes Antony.

CHARMIAN
          Not he. The Queen.

          Enter CLEOPATRA

CLEOPATRA
75   Saw you my lord?

ENOBARBUS
          No, lady.

CLEOPATRA
          Was he not here?

CHARMIAN
          No, madam.

CLEOPATRA
          He was disposed to mirth, but on the sudden
80   A Roman thought hath struck him.—Enobarbus!

ENOBARBUS
          Madam?

CLEOPATRA
          Seek him and bring him hither.—
          Where's Alexas?

ALEXAS
          Here at your service. My lord approaches.

          Enter ANTONY *with the* FIRST MESSENGER

Therefore, dear Isis, do the right thing and give him the fortune he deserves.

CHARMIAN

Amen.

ALEXAS

(to himself) See! If they could make me a cuckold, they'd whore themselves in order to see it done.

ENOBARBUS

Quiet! Here comes Antony.

CHARMIAN

It's not him; it's the Queen.

CLEOPATRA *enters.*

CLEOPATRA

Have you seen my lord?

ENOBARBUS

No, lady.

CLEOPATRA

Wasn't he here?

CHARMIAN

No, madam.

CLEOPATRA

He was in a good mood, and then suddenly he started thinking of Rome. Enobarbus?

ENOBARBUS

Madam?

CLEOPATRA

Find him and bring him here. Where's Alexas?

ALEXAS

Here, at your service. Here comes my lord.

ANTONY *and the* FIRST MESSENGER *enter.*

CLEOPATRA
85   We will not look upon him. Go with us.

Exeunt all but ANTONY *and the* FIRST MESSENGER

FIRST MESSENGER
      Fulvia thy wife first came into the field.

ANTONY
      Against my brother Lucius?

FIRST MESSENGER
      Ay.
      But soon that war had end, and the time's state
90   Made friends of them, joining their force 'gainst Caesar,
      Whose better issue in the war from Italy
      Upon the first encounter drave them.

ANTONY
      Well, what worst?

FIRST MESSENGER
      The nature of bad news infects the teller.

ANTONY
95   When it concerns the fool or coward. On.
      Things that are past are done, with me. 'Tis thus:
      Who tells me true, though in his tale lie death,
      I hear him as he flattered.

FIRST MESSENGER
                  Labienus—
      This is stiff news—hath with his Parthian force
100   Extended Asia: from Euphrates
      His conquering banner shook, from Syria
      To Lydia and to Ionia,
      Whilst—

CLEOPATRA

In the original text, Cleopatra refers to herself in the plural to denote her royal status.

I won't see him. Everyone come with me.

Everyone follows CLEOPATRA *out, leaving* ANTONY *and the* FIRST MESSENGER.

FIRST MESSENGER

Your wife, Fulvia, mustered her army first.

ANTONY

Against my brother Lucius?

FIRST MESSENGER

Yes. But that war ended as soon as circumstances made it advisable for them to join together against Caesar. But in their very first battle, Caesar won and drove them out of Italy.

ANTONY

Well, give me the worst news.

FIRST MESSENGER

The bearer of bad news is often blamed for it.

ANTONY

Only if the hearer is a fool or a coward. Go on. As far as I'm concerned, what's past is done. It's like this: as long as a person tells me the truth, even though it means my death, I will listen as though he praised me.

FIRST MESSENGER

Quintus Labienus was a Roman general charged with subduing Parthia, a hostile country in Asia Minor, and garnering Parthinian military support in the war against Antony and Octavius Caesar. When Cassius and Brutus were defeated, Labienus led the Parthians in a war against Rome, conquering some of the Roman territories in Asia along the way.

The news is disturbing. Labienus, with the army he led in Parthia, has conquered all of Asia, all the way to the Euphrates River, including Syria, Lydia, and Ionia, while—

ANTONY
"Antony," thou wouldst say.

FIRST MESSENGER
O my lord!

ANTONY
105   Speak to me home. Mince not the general tongue.
Name Cleopatra as she is called in Rome.
Rail thou in Fulvia's phrase, and taunt my faults
With such full license as both truth and malice
Have power to utter. Oh, then we bring forth weeds
110   When our quick minds lie still, and our ills told us
Is as our earing.

Enter SECOND MESSENGER

Fare thee well awhile.

FIRST MESSENGER
At your noble pleasure.

Exit FIRST MESSENGER

ANTONY
From Sicyon, how, the news? Speak there.

SECOND MESSENGER
The man from Sicyon—

ANTONY
Is there such an one?

SECOND MESSENGER
115   He stays upon your will.

ANTONY
Let him appear.

Exit SECOND MESSENGER

These strong Egyptian fetters I must break,
Or lose myself in dotage.

Enter THIRD MESSENGER, *with a letter*

What are you?

ANTONY

"While Antony . . ." is what you want to say.

FIRST MESSENGER

Oh, my lord!

ANTONY

Speak plainly. Don't tone down what the people are saying. Call Cleopatra what the Romans call her. Use Fulvia's abusive language. Freely scold me for my faults with as much severity as an enemy with truth on his side. It's easy to err when left to our own devices, but criticism helps us to see our faults and correct them.

A SECOND MESSENGER *enters.*

Good-bye for a while.

FIRST MESSENGER

I'll be at your service.

The FIRST MESSENGER *exits.*

ANTONY

What's the news from Sicyon. Tell me. ◄—— *Sicyon is the town in Greece where Antony left Fulvia.*

SECOND MESSENGER

The man from Sicyon—

ANTONY

Is he here?

SECOND MESSENGER

He's waiting outside.

ANTONY

Have him come in.

The SECOND MESSENGER *exits.*

(to himself) I must break Cleopatra's powerful hold over me or else I'll lose myself in foolish infatuation.

A THIRD MESSENGER *enters with a letter.*

What's your message?

THIRD MESSENGER
Fulvia thy wife is dead.

ANTONY
                                        Where died she?

THIRD MESSENGER
In Sicyon.
120   Her length of sickness, with what else more serious
Importeth thee to know, this bears.

He gives ANTONY *a letter*

ANTONY
                                        Forbear me.

Exit THIRD MESSENGER

(to himself) There's a great spirit gone! Thus did I desire it.
What our contempts doth often hurl from us
We wish it ours again. The present pleasure,
125   By revolution lowering, does become
The opposite of itself. She's good, being gone.
The hand could pluck her back that shoved her on.
I must from this enchanting Queen break off.
Ten thousand harms, more than the ills I know
130   My idleness doth hatch.—How now, Enobarbus!

Enter ENOBARBUS

ENOBARBUS
What's your pleasure, sir?

ANTONY
I must with haste from hence.

ENOBARBUS
Why, then, we kill all our women. We see how mortal an
unkindness is to them. If they suffer our departure, death's
135   the word.

THIRD MESSENGER

Your wife, Fulvia, is dead.

ANTONY

Where did she die?

THIRD MESSENGER

In Sicyon. In this letter you'll find details of her illness and other, more serious matters that concern you.

He hands the letter to **ANTONY**.

ANTONY

Leave me.

The **THIRD MESSENGER** *exits.*

(to himself) A great spirit has gone from the world! This is what I wanted. Once it's gone, the very thing we reject becomes what we desire. What's enjoyable one day becomes the opposite as time rolls around. Now that she's gone, I want her. Now I would call her back, though I pushed her away. I have to break from this beguiling Queen. The time I've wasted here has caused ten thousand more problems than the ones I know about. *(calling)* Are you there, Enobarbus?

ENOBARBUS *enters.*

ENOBARBUS

What would you like, sir?

ANTONY

I have to leave right away.

ENOBARBUS

That will kill our lovers. We know how much they suffer if we are unkind to them. If we leave, it will feel like nothing less than death to them.

ANTONY
> I must be gone.

ENOBARBUS
> Under a compelling occasion, let women die. It were pity to
> cast them away for nothing, though between them and a
> great cause they should be esteemed nothing. Cleopatra,
> catching but the least noise of this, dies instantly. I have
> seen her die twenty times upon far poorer moment. I do
> think there is mettle in death, which commits some loving
> act upon her, she hath such a celerity in dying.

ANTONY
> She is cunning past man's thought.

ENOBARBUS
> Alack, sir, no, her passions are made of nothing but the
> finest part of pure love. We cannot call her winds and waters
> sighs and tears. They are greater storms and tempests than
> almanacs can report. This cannot be cunning in her. If it be,
> she makes a shower of rain as well as Jove.

ANTONY
> Would I had never seen her!

ENOBARBUS
> O sir, you had then left unseen a wonderful piece of work,
> which not to have been blessed withal would have
> discredited your travel.

ANTONY
> Fulvia is dead.

ENOBARBUS
> Sir?

ANTONY
> Fulvia is dead.

ENOBARBUS
> Fulvia?

ANTONY
> Dead.

140
145
150
155

ANTONY

I must be gone.

ENOBARBUS

If it's that important, then let the women die. It would be a pity to throw them away for nothing, but if it's a matter of choosing between them and a great cause, then they're worthless. If Cleopatra hears even a breath of this, she'll die immediately. I've seen her claim to be dying twenty times before, and for far less reason. I think there must be something invigorating about death, since she dies with such enthusiasm.

ANTONY

She's more cunning than anyone can imagine.

ENOBARBUS

Jove = king of the Roman gods; commands thunder, lightning, and rain

Alas, sir, no, her feelings come from pure love, not cleverness. Her sighs and tears are like great winds and floods. She has more storms and tempests in her than a weather almanac. Her temper is not a trick or a skill—if it is, she can make it rain as well as Jove.

ANTONY

I wish I'd never seen her!

ENOBARBUS

Then you'd have missed an amazing piece of work, sir, and your trip would have been poorer for the loss.

ANTONY

Fulvia is dead.

ENOBARBUS

Pardon me?

ANTONY

Fulvia is dead.

ENOBARBUS

Fulvia?

ANTONY

Dead.

ENOBARBUS

Why, sir, give the gods a thankful sacrifice. When it
160   pleaseth their deities to take the wife of a man from him, it
shows to man the tailors of the earth, comforting therein,
that when old robes are worn out, there are members to
make new. If there were no more women but Fulvia, then
had you indeed a cut, and the case to be lamented. This grief
165   is crowned with consolation. Your old smock brings forth a
new petticoat, and indeed the tears live in an onion that
should water this sorrow.

ANTONY

The business she hath broached in the state
Cannot endure my absence.

ENOBARBUS

170   And the business you have broached here cannot be
without you, especially that of Cleopatra's, which wholly
depends on your abode.

ANTONY

No more light answers. Let our officers
Have notice what we purpose. I shall break
175   The cause of our expedience to the Queen
And get her leave to part. For not alone
The death of Fulvia, with more urgent touches,
Do strongly speak to us, but the letters too
Of many our contriving friends in Rome
180   Petition us at home. Sextus Pompeius
Hath given the dare to Caesar and commands
The empire of the sea. Our slippery people,
Whose love is never linked to the deserver
Till his deserts are past, begin to throw
185   Pompey the Great and all his dignities
Upon his son, who—high in name and power,
Higher than both in blood and life—stands up
For the main soldier, whose quality, going on,
The sides o' th' world may danger. Much is breeding

ENOBARBUS

> Then you should offer the gods a sacrifice to show
> your thanks. When a man's wife dies, he can be com-
> forted by the knowledge that there are replacements
> to be found. If Fulvia were the last woman on earth,
> there would be a reason to grieve. But in this way, grief
> and comfort appear together. The only kind of tears
> you should shed in this case are the kind you might get
> from holding an onion to your nose.

ANTONY

> I must go and continue the business Fulvia started.

ENOBARBUS

> The business you began here needs you as well—
> especially the business with Cleopatra, which only
> you can attend to.

ANTONY

> Enough of this frivolous talk. Give our officers
> notice of our intentions. I'll tell the Queen the reason
> for our quick departure and get her permission to
> leave. Fulvia's death and the pressing concerns related
> to it are not the only reasons I am eager to go; friends
> in Rome have also sent many letters advising my
> return. Sextus Pompeius has challenged Caesar. His
> fleet controls the sea. Our fickle citizens—who never
> reward service until that service is over—are now giv-
> ing all the rights and honors won by Pompey the
> Great to his son, Sextus. Sextus has great honor and
> power, and his spirit and energy are even greater, all of
> which makes him the most formidable soldier in the
> empire. The empire may be in danger if he's not
> restrained before he reaches his full potential. There
> are many troubles brewing now that have yet to
> become full-fledged threats.

190   Which, like the courser's hair, hath yet but life,
      And not a serpent's poison. Say our pleasure,
      To such whose place is under us, requires
      Our quick remove from hence.

ENOBARBUS
      I shall do 't.

                                                   Exeunt

This sentence refers to a popular belief of the time.

Like horse's hairs dropped in a bucket of water, they come alive like snakes but as yet they bear no poison. Relay our intentions to the officers who will be in charge of the move.

ENOBARBUS

I will.

They both exit.

ACT 1, SCENE 3

Enter CLEOPATRA, CHARMIAN, ALEXAS, *and* IRAS

CLEOPATRA
Where is he?

CHARMIAN
          I did not see him since.

CLEOPATRA
(to ALEXAS*)* See where he is, who's with him, what he does.
I did not send you. If you find him sad,
Say I am dancing. If in mirth, report
5 That I am sudden sick. Quick, and return.

                      Exit ALEXAS

CHARMIAN
Madam, methinks, if you did love him dearly,
You do not hold the method to enforce
The like from him.

CLEOPATRA
            What should I do I do not?

CHARMIAN
In each thing give him way. Cross him in nothing.

CLEOPATRA
10 Thou teachest like a fool the way to lose him.

CHARMIAN
Tempt him not so too far. I wish, forbear.
In time we hate that which we often fear.

Enter ANTONY

But here comes Antony.

CLEOPATRA
              I am sick and sullen.

ANTONY
I am sorry to give breathing to my purpose—

ACT 1, SCENE 3

CLEOPATRA, CHARMIAN, ALEXAS, *and* IRAS *enter.*

CLEOPATRA

Where is he?

CHARMIAN

I haven't seen him recently.

CLEOPATRA

(to ALEXAS*)* Find out where he is, who's with him, and what he's doing. Don't tell him I sent you. If he's sad, tell him I'm dancing. If he's happy, say that I've suddenly taken sick. Hurry, and come back.

ALEXAS *exits.*

CHARMIAN

Madam, I think if you love him so much, you aren't using the best way to get him to reciprocate.

CLEOPATRA

What should I do that I'm not doing?

CHARMIAN

Always give him his way. Never contradict him.

CLEOPATRA

You advise me like a fool. That's the way to lose him.

CHARMIAN

Don't push him too far. I wish you'd be patient. We come to hate that which controls us.

ANTONY *enters.*

But here comes Antony.

CLEOPATRA

I am sick and sullen.

ANTONY

I'm sorry to have to say this—

CLEOPATRA

15   Help me away, dear Charmian! I shall fall.
It cannot be thus long. The sides of nature
Will not sustain it.

ANTONY

Now, my dearest Queen—

CLEOPATRA

Pray you, stand farther from me.

ANTONY

What's the matter?

CLEOPATRA

I know by that same eye there's some good news.
20   What, says the married woman you may go?
Would she had never given you leave to come!
Let her not say 'tis I that keep you here.
I have no power upon you. Hers you are.

ANTONY

The gods best know—

CLEOPATRA

Oh never was there queen
25   So mightily betrayed! Yet at the first
I saw the treasons planted.

ANTONY

Cleopatra—

CLEOPATRA

Why should I think you can be mine, and true—
Though you in swearing shake the thronèd gods—
Who have been false to Fulvia? Riotous madness,
30   To be entangled with those mouth-made vows
Which break themselves in swearing!

ANTONY

Most sweet Queen—

CLEOPATRA

Nay, pray you, seek no color for your going,
But bid farewell and go. When you sued staying,

CLEOPATRA

Help me away from here, dear Charmian! I shall faint. I won't be able to go on this way much longer. Human nature isn't built to withstand this.

ANTONY

Now, my dearest Queen—

CLEOPATRA

Please, stand farther away from me.

ANTONY

What's the matter?

CLEOPATRA

I can see in your eyes there's been some good news. What, does your wife say you can come home? I wish she'd never let you come. Don't let her say I kept you. I have no power over you. You belong to her.

ANTONY

The gods know—

CLEOPATRA

Oh, never has a queen been so betrayed as I have been. I knew from the first it would be this way.

ANTONY

Cleopatra—

CLEOPATRA

How could I have ever thought that you would be faithful and true, even though your vows of love shook the heavens themselves—you, who were unfaithful to Fulvia? It was wild insanity to believe promises made by the mouth and not the heart. Such false vows are broken as soon as they are spoken.

ANTONY

Most sweet Queen—

CLEOPATRA

No, please don't try to excuse your departure. Just say good-bye and go. When you begged to stay, that was

Then was the time for words. No going then!
35   Eternity was in our lips and eyes,
Bliss in our brows' bent, none our parts so poor
But was a race of heaven. They are so still,
Or thou, the greatest soldier of the world,
Art turned the greatest liar.

ANTONY

How now, lady?

CLEOPATRA
40   I would I had thy inches. Thou shouldst know
There were a heart in Egypt.

ANTONY

Hear me, Queen:
The strong necessity of time commands
Our services awhile, but my full heart
Remains in use with you. Our Italy
45   Shines o'er with civil swords. Sextus Pompeius
Makes his approaches to the port of Rome.
Equality of two domestic powers
Breed scrupulous faction. The hated, grown to strength,
Are newly grown to love. The condemned Pompey,
50   Rich in his father's honor, creeps apace
Into the hearts of such as have not thrived
Upon the present state, whose numbers threaten;
And quietness, grown sick of rest, would purge
By any desperate change. My more particular,
55   And that which most with you should safe my going,
Is Fulvia's death.

CLEOPATRA
Though age from folly could not give me freedom,
It does from childishness. Can Fulvia die?

ANTONY
She's dead, my Queen.

He offers letters

the time for words. You didn't want to go then! You saw eternity in my lips and eyes, and happiness in the arch of my eyebrows. Then, all my parts seemed angelic to you. My features are still that beautiful—or else you, the greatest soldier in the world, have become the greatest liar by overpraising them.

ANTONY

What do you mean, lady?

CLEOPATRA

I wish I were as big and strong as you. Then you'd see the courage that lives in the Queen of Egypt.

ANTONY

Listen to me, Queen. There is an emergency I must take care of, but my whole heart will remain here with you. My Italy is full of civil war. Sextus Pompeius is sailing toward the port of Rome. When two domestic opponents are equally matched—as we are against Pompey—factions will form on the smallest of pretexts. When a formerly hated man grows powerful, he suddenly finds himself with many supporters. Pompey, who was once condemned, now wields his father's power, and all the citizens who have grievances against the government are joining him. Pompey's numbers are steadily growing, and the government is ready to do something desperate. But my personal motivation—and that which should move you most to sanction my departure—is that Fulvia is dead.

CLEOPATRA

I may not have outlived the foolishness of my youth, but I'm not that childishly naïve. Is it possible Fulvia is dead?

ANTONY

She's dead, my Queen.

He shows her the message.

60   Look here, and at thy sovereign leisure read
The garboils she awaked, at the last, best,
See when and where she died.

CLEOPATRA

                    O most false love!
Where be the sacred vials thou shouldst fill
With sorrowful water? Now I see, I see,
65   In Fulvia's death how mine received shall be.

ANTONY

Quarrel no more, but be prepared to know
The purposes I bear, which are or cease
As you shall give th' advice. By the fire
That quickens Nilus' slime, I go from hence
70   Thy soldier, servant, making peace or war
As thou affects.

CLEOPATRA

Cut my lace, Charmian, come!
But let it be. I am quickly ill, and well,
So Antony loves.

ANTONY

75   My precious Queen, forbear,
And give true evidence to his love which stands
An honorable trial.

CLEOPATRA

So Fulvia told me.
I prithee, turn aside and weep for her.
80   Then bid adieu to me, and say the tears
Belong to Egypt. Good now, play one scene
Of excellent dissembling, and let it look
Like perfect honor.

ANTONY

                 You'll heat my blood. No more.

CLEOPATRA

You can do better yet, but this is meetly.

ANTONY

85   Now, by my sword—

Look at this. Take your royal time and read about the quarrels she encouraged. And saving the best for last, read when and where she died.

CLEOPATRA

Ancient Romans often placed vials of tears inside their friends' funerary urns.

Oh, unfaithful lover! You should be filling vials with your tears. Seeing how you take Fulvia's death, I can see how you would react to mine.

ANTONY

Stop arguing and listen to my plans. Whether I go ahead with them or not is completely up to you. I swear by the sun that when I leave here, it will be as your faithful servant. I will make either peace or war, whichever you prefer.

CLEOPATRA

Cut my corset laces, Charmian, so I can breathe. Hurry! No, leave it alone. I waver easily between sickness and health. Just as Antony loves.

ANTONY

Control yourself, my precious Queen, and concede that my love is true. It has endured many genuine trials.

CLEOPATRA

That's what Fulvia told me. I beg you, turn away and cry for her. Then say good-bye to me and tell me those tears were for my benefit. Good. Now perform a scene for me, using your excellent skills of playacting, and pretend that you're being honorable and righteous.

ANTONY

You'll make me angry. No more of this.

CLEOPATRA

I know you can do better than that, but it'll do for now.

ANTONY

I swear by my sword—

CLEOPATRA
And target. Still he mends.
(*to* CHARMIAN) But this is not the best. Look, prithee,
Charmian,
How this Herculean Roman does become
The carriage of his chafe.

ANTONY
I'll leave you, lady.

CLEOPATRA
90   Courteous lord, one word.
Sir, you and I must part, but that's not it.
Sir, you and I have loved, but there's not it,
That you know well. Something it is I would—
Oh, my oblivion is a very Antony,
95   And I am all forgotten.

ANTONY
But that your royalty
Holds idleness your subject, I should take you
For idleness itself.

CLEOPATRA
'Tis sweating labor
To bear such idleness so near the heart
As Cleopatra this. But, sir, forgive me,
100   Since my becomings kill me when they do not
Eye well to you. Your honor calls you hence.
Therefore be deaf to my unpitied folly,
And all the gods go with you! Upon your sword
Sit laurel victory, and smooth success
105   Be strewed before your feet.

ANTONY
Let us go. Come.
Our separation so abides and flies
That thou, residing here, goes yet with me,
And I, hence fleeting, here remain with thee.
Away!

Exeunt

CLEOPATRA

> Swear by your shield, too! *(to* CHARMIAN*)* He's getting
> better, but still it's not his best. See, Charmian, how
> well this mighty Roman portrays anger?

ANTONY

> I'll leave you, lady.

CLEOPATRA

> Polite sir, let me say one thing. Sir, you and I must part
> company—no, that's not it. Sir, you and I were lov-
> ers—no, that's not it, either. You already know all that.
> There's something I'd like to—oh, I've forgotten what
> I wanted to say. Just as Antony has forgotten me.

ANTONY

> If you weren't the queen of immaturity, I'd think you
> were immaturity itself.

CLEOPATRA

> It's difficult to have such immaturity so close to my
> heart, but bear with me. Even the traits that become
> me most kill me when you don't approve of them.
> Your honor is the reason you are leaving. So I beg you
> not to listen to my foolishness. May the gods be with
> you. May your sword be victorious and everything
> you do succeed.

ANTONY

> Let's go. Come with me. Our imminent separation so
> occupies our thoughts that even though you stay here,
> you come with me, and even though I leave here, I stay
> with you.

> *They exit.*

ACT 1, SCENE 4

Enter OCTAVIUS CAESAR, *reading a letter,* LEPIDUS, *and their train*

CAESAR
You may see, Lepidus, and henceforth know,
It is not Caesar's natural vice to hate
Our great competitor. From Alexandria
This is the news: he fishes, drinks, and wastes
5   The lamps of night in revel; is not more manlike
Than Cleopatra, nor the queen of Ptolemy
More womanly than he; hardly gave audience, or
Vouchsafed to think he had partners. You shall find there
A man who is th' abstract of all faults
10 That all men follow.

LEPIDUS
                              I must not think there are
Evils enough to darken all his goodness.
His faults in him seem as the spots of heaven,
More fiery by night's blackness, hereditary
Rather than purchased, what he cannot change
15 Than what he chooses.

CAESAR
You are too indulgent. Let's grant, it is not
Amiss to tumble on the bed of Ptolemy,
To give a kingdom for a mirth, to sit
And keep the turn of tippling with a slave,
20 To reel the streets at noon, and stand the buffet
With knaves that smell of sweat. Say this becomes him—
As his composure must be rare indeed
Whom these things cannot blemish—yet must Antony
No way excuse his foils when we do bear
25 So great weight in his lightness. If he filled
His vacancy with his voluptuousness,
Full surfeits and the dryness of his bones

ACT 1, SCENE 4

OCTAVIUS CAESAR *enters, reading a letter, with* LEPIDUS *and their courtiers and attendants.*

CAESAR

Now you'll see, Lepidus, that I don't disdain our noble ally because of a personal whim. Here's the news from Alexandra: Antony fishes, drinks, and celebrates all night. He's become as frivolous and self-indulgent as Ptolemy's queen, Cleopatra. He rarely attends to his duties or acknowledges he has partners to be considered. Here's a man who is the epitome of all the vices known to man.

Ptolemy was Pharaoh of Egypt and Cleopatra's husband, now dead. (He was also her younger brother.)

LEPIDUS

I can't believe there could be enough vice in the world to outshine all the good in him. His faults stand out because they must be compared to all his virtues, like stars that shine brightly against the dark night sky. They're more likely to be the result of inherited weakness than independent choice.

CAESAR

You're too forgiving. Let's say, for argument's sake, that it's not improper to fool around with Ptolemy's wife, or to trade a kingdom for a joke. That it's fine to engage in drinking matches with inferiors, or stumble drunkenly through the streets in the middle of the day, or get into fist fights with sweaty servants. Even if we said that this behavior suits him—though only a man with a perfect character could avoid being disgraced by such antics—there's no excuse for the extra work we've had to take on while he's been off amusing himself. If he's been spending his leisure time in lustful pursuits, then he'll be punished with venereal dis-

Call on him for 't. But to confound such time
That drums him from his sport and speaks as loud
30 As his own state and ours, 'tis to be chid
As we rate boys who, being mature in knowledge,
Pawn their experience to their present pleasure
And so rebel to judgment.

Enter FIRST MESSENGER

LEPIDUS
                                        Here's more news.

FIRST MESSENGER
Thy biddings have been done, and every hour,
35 Most noble Caesar, shalt thou have report
How 'tis abroad. Pompey is strong at sea,
And it appears he is beloved of those
That only have feared Caesar. To the ports
The discontents repair, and men's reports
40 Give him much wronged.

CAESAR
                            I should have known no less.
It hath been taught us from the primal state
That he which is was wished until he were,
And the ebbed man, ne'er loved till ne'er worth love,
Comes deared by being lacked. This common body,
45 Like to a vagabond flag upon the stream,
Goes to and back, lackeying the varying tide
To rot itself with motion.

Enter SECOND MESSENGER

SECOND MESSENGER
Caesar, I bring thee word
Menecrates and Menas, famous pirates,
50 Make the sea serve them, which they ear and wound
With keels of every kind. Many hot inroads

eases, and that's his business. But he's wasting time and resources vital to our cause and endangering both his position and ours. He should be chastised, like any boy who knows what's right but chooses to satisfy his desires regardless.

The FIRST MESSENGER *enters.*

LEPIDUS

Here's more news.

FIRST MESSENGER

We've followed your commands, lord Caesar. You shall have hourly updates regarding the situation at sea. Pompey has a strong navy. All the people who only stayed with you out of fear are gathering at the port to join him, in the opinion he's been treated unfairly.

CAESAR

I should have known it. It's been this way ever since the first government was organized. People will transfer their support to a strong figure until he becomes their actual leader. Then they will value their former leader, even though the loss of their support has made him powerless. The common crowd changes like the tide, to and fro, serving whoever is on the rise. Their power is worn away by their fickleness.

The SECOND MESSENGER *enters.*

SECOND MESSENGER

Caesar, I have news about Menecrates and Menas, notorious pirates who prowl the sea in a variety of ships. They've made many raids upon Italy—and the

They make in Italy—the borders maritime
Lack blood to think on 't—and flush youth revolt.
No vessel can peep forth, but 'tis as soon
55   Taken as seen, for Pompey's name strikes more
Than could his war resisted.

                                             Exit

CAESAR
                                   Antony,
Leave thy lascivious wassails. When thou once
Wast beaten from Modena, where thou slew'st
Hirtius and Pansa, consuls, at thy heel
60   Did famine follow, whom thou fought'st against,
Though daintily brought up, with patience more
Than savages could suffer. Thou didst drink
The stale of horses and the gilded puddle
Which beasts would cough at. Thy palate then did deign
65   The roughest berry on the rudest hedge.
Yea, like the stag, when snow the pasture sheets,
The barks of trees thou browsèd. On the Alps
It is reported thou didst eat strange flesh,
Which some did die to look on. And all this—
70   It wounds thine honor that I speak it now—
Was borne so like a soldier, that thy cheek
So much as lanked not.

LEPIDUS
'Tis pity of him.

CAESAR
Let his shames quickly
75   Drive him to Rome. 'Tis time we twain
Did show ourselves i' th' field, and to that end
Assemble we immediate council. Pompey
Thrives in our idleness.

naval patrols go pale at even the thought of resisting them. The young, energetic men are joining Pompey. These pirates can capture a ship as soon as it leaves the harbor, since the simple mention of the name "Pompey" carries as much power as a fleet of troops in battle.

SECOND MESSENGER *exits.*

CAESAR

Antony, it's time to stop your wild hedonism. When you were defeated at the battle of Modena—where you killed the consuls, Hirtius and Pansa—and then driven away, you had to face hunger and thirst. And even though you were brought up as a gentleman, you patiently tolerated more hardships than savages could withstand. You drank horses' urine and water from scum-covered puddles that even animals would refuse. Though you were used to the finest foods, you didn't turn up your nose at the bitterest berries on the thorniest bushes. You even ate bark from trees, as deer do in winter. Going over the Alps, you ate strange meat that some men would rather die than consume. And you went through all this—the comparison between then and now shames you—in such a soldier-like way that you didn't seem to suffer at all.

LEPIDUS

It's too bad.

CAESAR

Let's hope his sense of shame will send him back to Rome quickly. It's time that we brought our armies into the field. Let's call a council of war immediately. Pompey is making the most of our absence.

LEPIDUS
                              Tomorrow, Caesar,
I shall be furnished to inform you rightly
80   Both what by sea and land I can be able
To front this present time.

CAESAR
                              Till which encounter
It is my business too. Farewell.

LEPIDUS
Farewell, my lord. What you shall know meantime
Of stirs abroad, I shall beseech you, sir,
85   To let me be partaker.

CAESAR
Doubt not, sir. I knew it for my bond.

                                             Exeunt

LEPIDUS

Tomorrow, Caesar, I'll be able to tell you what land and sea forces I can raise for this war.

CAESAR

I'll be getting my own figures together in the meantime. Good-bye.

LEPIDUS

Good-bye, my lord. If you receive any more news, please share it with me.

CAESAR

Don't worry, that goes without saying.

They exit.

ACT 1, SCENE 5

Enter CLEOPATRA, CHARMIAN, IRAS, *and* MARDIAN

CLEOPATRA
Charmian!

CHARMIAN
Madam?

CLEOPATRA
Ha, ha! Give me to drink mandragora.

CHARMIAN
Why, madam?

CLEOPATRA
5   That I might sleep out this great gap of time
My Antony is away.

CHARMIAN
You think of him too much.

CLEOPATRA
Oh, 'tis treason!

CHARMIAN
                        Madam, I trust, not so.

CLEOPATRA
Thou, eunuch Mardian!

MARDIAN
                        What's your highness' pleasure?

CLEOPATRA
10   Not now to hear thee sing. I take no pleasure
In aught an eunuch has. 'Tis well for thee
That, being unseminared, thy freer thoughts
May not fly forth of Egypt. Hast thou affections?

MARDIAN
Yes, gracious madam.

CLEOPATRA
15   Indeed?

ACT 1, SCENE 5

CLEOPATRA, CHARMIAN, IRAS, *and* MARDIAN *enter.*

CLEOPATRA

Charmian!

CHARMIAN

Madam?

CLEOPATRA

mandragora =
narcotic syrup

Ah, give me some mandragora to drink.

CHARMIAN

Why, madam?

CLEOPATRA

So I can sleep away the time while my Antony is gone.

CHARMIAN

You think about him too much.

CLEOPATRA

That's treason!

CHARMIAN

I hope not, Madam.

CLEOPATRA

Eunuch! Mardian!

MARDIAN

What can I do for your highness?

CLEOPATRA

I don't want to hear you sing. I'm not interested in anything a eunuch can do. It's a good thing for you that, being castrated, you can better concentrate on my needs. Do you have desires?

MARDIAN

Yes, dear madam.

CLEOPATRA

Indeed?

MARDIAN

Not in deed, madam, for I can do nothing
But what indeed is honest to be done.
Yet have I fierce affections, and think
What Venus did with Mars.

CLEOPATRA

O Charmian,

20   Where think'st thou he is now? Stands he or sits he?
Or does he walk? Or is he on his horse?
O happy horse, to bear the weight of Antony!
Do bravely, horse, for wott'st thou whom thou mov'st?
The demi-Atlas of this earth, the arm
25   And burgonet of men. He's speaking now,
Or murmuring "Where's my serpent of old Nile?"
For so he calls me. Now I feed myself
With most delicious poison. Think on me,
That am with Phoebus' amorous pinches black
30   And wrinkled deep in time. Broad-fronted Caesar,
When thou wast here above the ground, I was
A morsel for a monarch. And great Pompey
Would stand and make his eyes grow in my brow.
There would he anchor his aspect, and die
35   With looking on his life.

Enter ALEXAS

ALEXAS

Sovereign of Egypt, hail!

CLEOPATRA

How much unlike art thou Mark Antony!
Yet, coming from him, that great med'cine hath
With his tinct gilded thee.
40   How goes it with my brave Mark Antony?

ALEXAS

Last thing he did, dear Queen,
He kissed—the last of many doubled kisses—

MARDIAN

Venus, goddess of love, and Mars, god of war, were legendary lovers.

Well, not in deed, madam, since I can't do anything unchaste. But I do have intense passions—and I do think about what Venus did with Mars.

CLEOPATRA

Oh, Charmian, where do you think he is now? Is he standing or sitting? Or is he walking? Or is he on his horse? Oh, how fortunate that horse is to have Antony on him. Do well, horse. Do you know whom it is you carry? A man who carries responsibility for a third of the world on his shoulders. He's speaking now, or perhaps he's whispering, "Where's my serpent of the Nile?" For that's his pet name for me. I'm killing myself with this provocative speculation . . . Are you thinking about me? Even though I've been darkened by the sun and wrinkled with age? Caesar, with your broad forehead, when you were alive, I was the perfect young consort for a king. And powerful Pompey used to stare at me as if he were frozen in time.

Referring to two previous lovers, Julius Caesar and Gneius Pompey (son of Pompey the Great and elder brother of Sextus Pompeius).

ALEXAS *enters.*

ALEXAS

Queen of Egypt, greetings!

CLEOPATRA

You are nothing like Mark Antony! But since you come from him, you're saturated with his healing spirit. How does it go with my magnificent Mark Antony?

ALEXAS

The last thing he did before sending me off, dear Queen, was to kiss—the last of many such kisses—

This orient pearl.

He gives a pearl.

His speech sticks in my heart.

CLEOPATRA
Mine ear must pluck it thence.

ALEXAS
"Good friend," quoth he,
45 "Say the firm Roman to great Egypt sends
This treasure of an oyster, at whose foot,
To mend the petty present, I will piece
Her opulent throne with kingdoms. All the East,
Say thou, shall call her mistress." So he nodded,
50 And soberly did mount an arm-gaunt steed,
Who neighed so high that what I would have spoke
Was beastly dumbed by him.

CLEOPATRA
What was he, sad or merry?

ALEXAS
Like to the time o' th' year between the extremes
55 Of hot and cold, he was nor sad nor merry.

CLEOPATRA
O well-divided disposition! Note him,
Note him, good Charmian, 'tis the man, but note him.
He was not sad, for he would shine on those
That make their looks by his. He was not merry,
60 Which seemed to tell them his remembrance lay
In Egypt with his joy, but between both.
O heavenly mingle! Be'st thou sad or merry,
The violence of either thee becomes,
So does it no man else.—Mett'st thou my posts?

ALEXAS
65 Ay, madam, twenty several messengers.
Why do you send so thick?

this Indian pearl for you.

He gives CLEOPATRA *a pearl.*

His speech is stored in my heart.

CLEOPATRA

My ear must pull it out.

ALEXAS

"Good friend," he said, "say that the faithful Roman sends an oyster's treasure to the great Queen of Egypt, and that he plans to enhance this meager gift by adding new kingdoms to her empire. Tell her that the entire East shall call her Queen." Then he nodded and solemnly mounted an armored warhorse, which neighed so loudly it effectively silenced anything I might have said in reply.

CLEOPATRA

Was he sad or happy?

ALEXAS

He was like that time of year halfway between the extremes of hot and cold: he was neither sad nor happy.

CLEOPATRA

Oh, what an even disposition he has! Observe, observe good Charmian! That's exactly how he is! Just notice. He wasn't sad, because he knows that his disposition affects others. He wasn't merry, because to be merry would indicate that he had forgotten his love in Egypt. He was somewhere in the middle, between them . . . Oh, heavenly mixture! Whether you are sad or merry, the intensity of either suits you like no one else . . . Did you meet my messengers on your way here?

ALEXAS

Yes, madam, twenty different messengers. Why did you send so many?

CLEOPATRA
                              Who's born that day
When I forget to send to Antony
Shall die a beggar. Ink and paper, Charmian.
Welcome, my good Alexas. Did I, Charmian,
70 Ever love Caesar so?

CHARMIAN
                        Oh, that brave Caesar!

CLEOPATRA
Be choked with such another emphasis!
Say, "the brave Antony."

CHARMIAN
                        The valiant Caesar!

CLEOPATRA
By Isis, I will give thee bloody teeth
If thou with Caesar paragon again
75 My man of men.

CHARMIAN
                    By your most gracious pardon,
I sing but after you.

CLEOPATRA
                    My salad days,
When I was green in judgment, cold in blood,
To say as I said then. *(to everyone)* But, come, away.
(to **CHARMIAN***)* Get me ink and paper.
80 He shall have every day a several greeting,
Or I'll unpeople Egypt.

                                        Exeunt

CLEOPATRA

Whoever is born on a day I forget to send a message to Antony will die a beggar. Bring ink and paper, Charmian. Welcome, my good Alexas. Charmian, did I ever love Caesar as much as this?

CHARMIAN

Oh, that splendid Caesar!

CLEOPATRA

May you choke on any other sentiments like that! Say, "That splendid Antony."

CHARMIAN

The courageous Caesar!

CLEOPATRA

By Isis, I'll give you bloody teeth if you ever compare Caesar with Antony, my best man among men.

CHARMIAN

Pardon me, but I'm just repeating what you yourself have said.

CLEOPATRA

That was when I was young and inexperienced and didn't know what passion was. *(to everyone)* But come. *(to* CHARMIAN*)* Go get me ink and paper. He shall have different messages every day if I have to depopulate Egypt to send them.

They all exit.

ACT TWO

SCENE 1

Enter POMPEY, MENECRATES, *and* MENAS, *in warlike manner*

POMPEY
    If the great gods be just, they shall assist
    The deeds of justest men.

MENAS
                      Know, worthy Pompey,
    That what they do delay, they not deny.

POMPEY
    Whiles we are suitors to their throne, decays
⁵   The thing we sue for.

MENAS
                 We, ignorant of ourselves,
    Beg often our own harms, which the wise powers
    Deny us for our good, so find we profit
    By losing of our prayers.

POMPEY
                 I shall do well.
    The people love me, and the sea is mine.
¹⁰   My powers are crescent, and my auguring hope
    Says it will come to th' full. Mark Antony
    In Egypt sits at dinner, and will make
    No wars without doors. Caesar gets money where
    He loses hearts. Lepidus flatters both,
¹⁵   Of both is flattered, but he neither loves,
    Nor either cares for him.

MENAS
                Caesar and Lepidus
    Are in the field. A mighty strength they carry.

ACT TWO
SCENE 1

POMPEY, MENECRATES, *and* MENAS *enter, dressed for battle.*

POMPEY

If the great gods are just, they will help the most honest men.

MENAS

You should know, noble Pompey, that although the gods may delay action, that doesn't mean they will necessarily refuse their help.

POMPEY

But while we pray and wait for that help, the cause we petition for may be lost.

MENAS

Sometimes we don't know what's best for us and ask for things that may harm us. In that case, the wise gods deny our prayers for our own good.

POMPEY

I'll do well. The people are on my side, and I'm in charge of the sea. My forces are growing, and everything I know tells me it's all coming together. Mark Antony is at dinner in Egypt and won't be going outside to make war. Caesar loses supporters wherever he raises money. Lepidus flatters both of them, as they flatter him, but he doesn't love them, and they don't love him.

MENAS

Caesar and Lepidus are organizing their military operation. They have a massive army.

POMPEY
    Where have you this? 'Tis false.

MENAS
                             From Silvius, sir.

POMPEY
    He dreams. I know they are in Rome together
20   Looking for Antony. But all the charms of love,
    Salt Cleopatra, soften thy wanned lip!
    Let witchcraft join with beauty, lust with both.
    Tie up the libertine in a field of feasts,
    Keep his brain fuming. Epicurean cooks,
25   Sharpen with cloyless sauce his appetite,
    That sleep and feeding may prorogue his honor
    Even till a Lethe'd dulness—

Enter **VARRIUS**

                         How now, Varrius?

VARRIUS
    This is most certain that I shall deliver:
    Mark Antony is every hour in Rome
30   Expected. Since he went from Egypt 'tis
    A space for farther travel.

POMPEY
    I could have given less matter
    A better ear.—Menas, I did not think
    This amorous surfeiter would have donned his helm
35   For such a petty war. His soldiership
    Is twice the other twain. But let us rear
    The higher our opinion, that our stirring
    Can from the lap of Egypt's widow pluck
    The ne'er lust-wearied Antony.

MENAS
                        I cannot hope
40   Caesar and Antony shall well greet together.
    His wife that's dead did trespasses to Caesar.

POMPEY

Where did you hear this? It's not true.

MENAS

From Silvius, sir.

POMPEY

He's dreaming. I know they're in Rome together, hoping for Antony to return. Lecherous Cleopatra, may all the charms of love soften those withered lips! Join your witchcraft with your beauty, and let Antony's lust combine with both. Keep this libertine occupied with endless debauchery. Keep his brain drunk and his appetite unsatisfied, so that sleeping and eating make him drowsy and forgetful of his duties, like the Lethe does.

Lethe = mythical river of the underworld; to drink from it brought forgetfulness

VARRIUS *enters.*

What's the news, Varrius?

VARRIUS

This news is absolutely true: Mark Antony is expected to arrive in Rome at any hour now. In the time since he left Egypt, he could have traveled an even longer distance.

POMPEY

I would have listened to less important news with greater enthusiasm. Menas, I had no idea this amorous glutton would have put on his helmet for such an insignificant war. His military ability is double that of the other two. We must form a better opinion of ourselves if our uprising can pull the insatiable Antony's attention away from that Egyptian widow.

MENAS

I don't expect Caesar and Antony will have a very friendly reunion. Antony's dead wife raised an army

His brother warred upon him, although, I think,
Not moved by Antony.

POMPEY

                                        I know not, Menas,
How lesser enmities may give way to greater.
45 Were 't not that we stand up against them all,
'Twere pregnant they should square between themselves,
For they have entertainèd cause enough
To draw their swords. But how the fear of us
May cement their divisions and bind up
50 The petty difference, we yet not know.
Be 't as our gods will have 't. It only stands
Our lives upon to use our strongest hands.
Come, Menas.

                                        Exeunt

against him, as did his brother, though I don't think Antony instigated it.

POMPEY

Menas, I don't understand how minor quarrels can be superseded by greater ones. If it weren't for the fact that we oppose all three of them together, they'd be fighting each other. They certainly have enough provocation. But it's possible the fear of us may mend their petty differences, though how that will work out, we cannot say. It will be as the gods see fit. In any case, our survival depends on putting together the strongest force possible. Let's go, Menas.

They exit.

ACT 2, SCENE 2

Enter ENOBARBUS *and* LEPIDUS

LEPIDUS
Good Enobarbus, 'tis a worthy deed,
And shall become you well, to entreat your captain
To soft and gentle speech.

ENOBARBUS
                    I shall entreat him
To answer like himself. If Caesar move him,
5   Let Antony look over Caesar's head
And speak as loud as Mars. By Jupiter,
Were I the wearer of Antonio's beard,
I would not shave 't today.

LEPIDUS
'Tis not a time for private stomaching.

ENOBARBUS
10   Every time serves for the matter that is then born in 't.

LEPIDUS
But small to greater matters must give way.

ENOBARBUS
Not if the small come first.

LEPIDUS
Your speech is passion. But pray you stir
No embers up. Here comes the noble Antony.

Enter ANTONY *and* VENTIDIUS

ENOBARBUS
15   And yonder, Caesar.

Enter OCTAVIUS CAESAR, MECAENAS, *and* AGRIPPA

ACT 2, SCENE 2

ENOBARBUS *and* LEPIDUS *enter.*

LEPIDUS

Good Enobarbus, you would be doing a very good thing if you advised your captain to speak calmly and quietly.

ENOBARBUS

I will advise him to speak as he usually does. If Caesar makes him mad, let Antony stand tall and speak as loudly as Mars, the god of war. By Jupiter, if I were Antony, I wouldn't shave my beard today. I'd leave it long and dare Caesar to insult me by pulling on it, just so I could fight him.

LEPIDUS

This is not the time for dwelling on personal grievances.

ENOBARBUS

It's always appropriate to deal with matters as they arise.

LEPIDUS

But major issues must come before minor ones.

ENOBARBUS

Not if the minor ones come up first.

LEPIDUS

You speak out of passion, but I beg you not to stir things up. Here comes the noble Antony.

ANTONY *and* VENTIDIUS *enter.*

ENOBARBUS

And there comes Caesar.

CAESAR, MAECENAS, *and* AGRIPPA *enter from another door.*

ANTONY
(to VENTIDIUS*)* If we compose well here, to Parthia.
Hark, Ventidius.

They talk aside

CAESAR
(to MECAENAS*)* I do not know, Maecenas. Ask Agrippa.

LEPIDUS
(to CAESAR *and* ANTONY*)* Noble friends,

20   That which combined us was most great, and let not
A leaner action rend us. What's amiss,
May it be gently heard. When we debate
Our trivial difference loud, we do commit
Murder in healing wounds. Then, noble partners,

25   The rather for I earnestly beseech,
Touch you the sourest points with sweetest terms,
Nor curstness grow to th' matter.

ANTONY
                                    'Tis spoken well.
Were we before our armies, and to fight,
I should do thus.

Flourish

CAESAR
30   Welcome to Rome.

ANTONY
Thank you.

CAESAR
Sit.

ANTONY
Sit, sir.

CAESAR
Nay, then.

ANTONY

(to VENTIDIUS*)* If we can come to an agreement here, we'll move on to Parthia. Listen, Ventidius.

They talk privately together.

CAESAR

(to MAECENAS*)* I don't know, Maecenas. Ask Agrippa.

LEPIDUS

(to CAESAR *and* ANTONY*)* Good friends, the cause that joined us was noble. Don't let some petty quarrel tear us apart. Let's discuss this calmly. When we argue our differences with raised voices, we do more harm than good. So I plead with you to use reasonable words as you discuss these unreasonable deeds, and don't lose your tempers.

ANTONY

You're right. If we were in front of our armies, about to fight, I would do this.

A trumpet fanfare.

CAESAR

Welcome to Rome.

ANTONY

Thank you.

CAESAR

Have a seat.

ANTONY

After you.

CAESAR

No, after you.

They sit

ANTONY
35   I learn, you take things ill which are not so,
        Or being, concern you not.

CAESAR
                                    I must be laughed at
        If or for nothing or a little, I
        Should say myself offended, and with you
        Chiefly i' th' world; more laughed at, that I should
40   Once name you derogately, when to sound your name
        It not concerned me.

ANTONY
        My being in Egypt, Caesar, what was 't to you?

CAESAR
        No more than my residing here at Rome
        Might be to you in Egypt. Yet if you there
45   Did practice on my state, your being in Egypt
        Might be my question.

ANTONY
                                    How intend you, "practiced"?

CAESAR
        You may be pleased to catch at mine intent
        By what did here befall me. Your wife and brother
        Made wars upon me, and their contestation
50   Was theme for you. You were the word of war.

ANTONY
        You do mistake your business. My brother never
        Did urge me in his act. I did inquire it,
        And have my learning from some true reports
        That drew their swords with you. Did he not rather
55   Discredit my authority with yours,
        And make the wars alike against my stomach,
        Having alike your cause? Of this my letters
        Before did satisfy you. If you'll patch a quarrel,

They sit.

ANTONY

I hear you've interpreted some of my actions as being improper, when they weren't improper at all—or if they were, their impropriety didn't concern you.

CAESAR

I should be ridiculed if I were offended so easily—and laughed at even more for speaking of you disrespect-fully, when I had no reason to speak of you at all.

ANTONY

Caesar, what did my stay in Egypt have to do with you?

CAESAR

No more than my staying here in Rome might mean to you in Egypt. But if you conspired against my position while you were there, I might be interested in the reason for your stay in Egypt.

ANTONY

How do you mean, "conspired"?

CAESAR

You can judge for yourself what I mean. Your wife and brother led troops against me, claiming to be fighting in your name. They said they were acting for you.

ANTONY

You're mistaken. My brother didn't use my name to justify his rebellion. I talked to some reliable partici-pants in that battle. On the contrary, his fight was with both of us. He rejected my authority as much as yours. Since you and I share a common cause, wouldn't his actions against you be hostile to me as well? I've already sent the proof in my letters. If you want to pick a fight,

As matter whole you have to make it with,
60   It must not be with this.

CAESAR
                              You praise yourself
By laying defects of judgment to me, but
You patched up your excuses.

ANTONY
                                    Not so, not so.
I know you could not lack, I am certain on 't,
Very necessity of this thought, that I,
65   Your partner in the cause 'gainst which he fought,
Could not with graceful eyes attend those wars
Which fronted mine own peace. As for my wife,
I would you had her spirit in such another.
The third o' th' world is yours, which with a snaffle
70   You may pace easy, but not such a wife.

ENOBARBUS
Would we had all such wives, that the men might go to wars
with the women!

ANTONY
So much uncurbable, her garboils, Caesar,
Made out of her impatience—which not wanted
75   Shrewdness of policy too—I grieving grant
Did you too much disquiet. For that you must
But say I could not help it.

CAESAR
                              I wrote to you
When rioting in Alexandria. You
Did pocket up my letters and with taunts
80   Did gibe my missive out of audience.

ANTONY
                                        Sir,
He fell upon me ere admitted, then.
Three kings I had newly feasted, and did want
Of what I was i' th' morning. But next day
I told him of myself, which was as much

you'll have to find a more substantial excuse.

CAESAR

You defend yourself by blaming my judgment, but you're just making up feeble excuses.

ANTONY

Not true, not true. You know I would never approve a war against my own cause. As for my wife, if only you had such a wife. It's easier to rule a third of the world than a wife like that.

ENOBARBUS

We should all have wives like that. Then the women could go to war with the men.

ANTONY

I had no control over her uprisings, Caesar, which arose from her impatience—and were shrewdly undertaken, as well. I'm sorry she caused you so much trouble. But you can't blame me for her offenses.

CAESAR

I sent you a letter while you were carousing in Alexandria. You put my letters in your pocket without reading them and then mocked my messenger out of the room.

ANTONY

Sir, he burst into the room without invitation, just after I had come from an important banquet with three kings. I was not myself, as a result of the wine. The next day I explained all this to him, which was as good

85   As to have asked him pardon. Let this fellow
    Be nothing of our strife. If we contend,
    Out of our question wipe him.

CAESAR
                          You have broken
    The article of your oath, which you shall never
    Have tongue to charge me with.

LEPIDUS
90   Soft, Caesar.

ANTONY
    No, Lepidus, let him speak.
    The honor is sacred which he talks on now,
    Supposing that I lacked it.—But, on, Caesar.
    The article of my oath?

CAESAR
95   To lend me arms and aid when I required them,
    The which you both denied.

ANTONY
                    Neglected, rather,
    And then when poisoned hours had bound me up
    From mine own knowledge. As nearly as I may
    I'll play the penitent to you, but mine honesty
100   Shall not make poor my greatness nor my power
    Work without it. Truth is that Fulvia,
    To have me out of Egypt, made wars here,
    For which myself, the ignorant motive, do
    So far ask pardon as befits mine honor
105   To stoop in such a case.

LEPIDUS
                    'Tis noble spoken.

MAECENAS
    If it might please you to enforce no further
    The griefs between ye, to forget them quite
    Were to remember that the present need
    Speaks to atone you.

as begging his pardon. Let's not fight over this fellow. If we must argue, let us remove him from our arguments.

CAESAR

You've broken the terms of our sworn agreement. You will never be able to say the same about me.

LEPIDUS

Easy, Caesar.

ANTONY

No, Lepidus, let him say what's on his mind. Now he slanders my honor, which is sacred to me. Go on, Caesar. What part of the agreement did I break?

CAESAR

You agreed to send me troops and weapons when I needed them. You refused me both.

ANTONY

I overlooked your request, but I did not deny it. Your request came at a time when the poisonous effects of reveling caused me to be unaware of my own actions. I will apologize as much as is appropriate, but my apology will not diminish my great stature—or if I am denied that honor, I will withhold my military might. The truth is that to get me out of Egypt, Fulvia provoked riots here. And though I am only indirectly the cause of all this trouble, I ask your pardon to the extent that my honor permits me to lower myself in such a situation.

LEPIDUS

Spoken like a gentleman.

MAECENAS

If it's okay with you, you should not press your grievances any further, but realize that the current situation should be enough to reconcile you.

LEPIDUS
                    Worthily spoken, Maecenas.

ENOBARBUS
110   Or, if you borrow one another's love for the instant, you
        may, when you hear no more words of Pompey, return it
        again. You shall have time to wrangle in when you have
        nothing else to do.

ANTONY
        Thou art a soldier only. Speak no more.

ENOBARBUS
115   That truth should be silent I had almost forgot.

ANTONY
        You wrong this presence. Therefore speak no more.

ENOBARBUS
        Go to, then. Your considerate stone.

CAESAR
        I do not much dislike the matter, but
        The manner of his speech, for 't cannot be
120   We shall remain in friendship, our conditions
        So diff'ring in their acts. Yet if I knew
        What hoop should hold us stanch, from edge to edge
        O' th' world I would pursue it.

AGRIPPA
        Give me leave, Caesar.

CAESAR
125   Speak, Agrippa.

AGRIPPA
        Thou hast a sister by the mother's side,
        Admired Octavia. Great Mark Antony
        Is now a widower.

LEPIDUS

> Well put, Maecenas.

ENOBARBUS

> Or you can pretend to settle your differences until this matter with Pompey is finished. You can argue as much as you like when there's nothing else to do.

ANTONY

> You are only a soldier. Be quiet.

ENOBARBUS

> Oh, I'd forgotten that no one's supposed to speak the truth.

ANTONY

> It's not appropriate for a soldier to be part of a discussion among noblemen. Don't speak any further.

ENOBARBUS

> As you please. I'll pretend to be a conscious stone, and think without speaking.

CAESAR

> I agree with what he says, though I don't care for the way he says it. It's not possible for us to be friends anymore. We're too different, in both our dispositions and actions. But if there were something that could join us together again, I would go to the ends of the world to find it.

AGRIPPA

> May I speak, Caesar.

CAESAR

> What is it, Agrippa?

AGRIPPA

> You have a beautiful half-sister, Octavia. Great Mark Antony is a widower now.

CAESAR
                              Say not so, Agrippa.
If Cleopatra heard you, your reproof
130   Were well deserved of rashness.

ANTONY
I am not married, Caesar. Let me hear
Agrippa further speak.

AGRIPPA
To hold you in perpetual amity,
To make you brothers, and to knit your hearts
135   With an unslipping knot, take Antony
Octavia to his wife, whose beauty claims
No worse a husband than the best of men,
Whose virtue and whose general graces speak
That which none else can utter. By this marriage,
140   All little jealousies, which now seem great,
And all great fears, which now import their dangers,
Would then be nothing. Truths would be tales,
Where now half-tales be truths. Her love to both
Would each to other and all loves to both
145   Draw after her. Pardon what I have spoke,
For 'tis a studied, not a present thought,
By duty ruminated.

ANTONY
                              Will Caesar speak?

CAESAR
Not till he hears how Antony is touched
With what is spoke already.

ANTONY
150   What power is in Agrippa
If I would say, "Agrippa, be it so,"
To make this good?

CAESAR
                              The power of Caesar, and
His power unto Octavia.

CAESAR

You'd better not make that suggestion, Agrippa. If Cleopatra heard you, you would be well punished for your audacity.

ANTONY

It's true I'm not married, Caesar. Let me hear what Agrippa has to say.

AGRIPPA

If Antony were to take Octavia as his wife, you two would be bound in eternal friendship. As brothers, your hearts would be tied together in an unbreakable knot. She is beautiful enough for the best of men. Her virtue and grace are unparalleled. With this marriage, all the petty jealousies that now seem huge, and all the great fears that are dangerous in themselves, would disappear. People would become used to speaking the truth rather than gossip. Since she would love both of you, you two would be joined in that love. Excuse my bluntness. This is not a spur-of-the-moment suggestion. I have been considering this for some time, in my duties to both of you.

ANTONY

What do you say, Caesar?

CAESAR

I'd rather hear your reaction to this first.

ANTONY

If I said to Agrippa, "I agree. Make it happen," does Agrippa have the power to make it so?

CAESAR

He has both my power and my influence over Octavia.

ANTONY

                                        May I never
To this good purpose, that so fairly shows,
155   Dream of impediment! Let me have thy hand
Further this act of grace, and from this hour
The heart of brothers govern in our loves
And sway our great designs!

CAESAR

                                        There's my hand.

They clasp hands

A sister I bequeath you whom no brother
160   Did ever love so dearly. Let her live
To join our kingdoms and our hearts, and never
Fly off our loves again!

LEPIDUS

                                        Happily, amen!

ANTONY

I did not think to draw my sword 'gainst Pompey,
For he hath laid strange courtesies and great
165   Of late upon me. I must thank him only,
Lest my remembrance suffer ill report;
At heel of that, defy him.

LEPIDUS

                                        Time calls upon 's.
Of us must Pompey presently be sought,
Or else he seeks out us.

ANTONY

170   Where lies he?

CAESAR

About the Mount Misena.

ANTONY

What is his strength by land?

ANTONY

I wouldn't dream of opposing such an obviously promising idea. Let's shake on it. If you go through with this plan, from now on we'll be brothers, and our love for one another will guide our actions.

CAESAR

Here's my hand.

They shake hands.

I give you a sister whom I love more than a brother ever loved any sister. She will be the bond that joins our kingdoms and our hearts. We'll never fight again.

LEPIDUS

I'm happy to say "amen" to that!

ANTONY

I didn't think I would ever fight Pompey. He's shown me unusual deference lately, and I must repay his favors or risk a reputation for ingratitude. That done, I can turn against him.

LEPIDUS

There isn't much time. Either we go after Pompey or he'll come after us.

ANTONY

Where is he now?

CAESAR

Near Mt. Misena.

Hilly port town south of Rome

ANTONY

How large is his land army?

CAESAR
Great and increasing.
But by sea he is an absolute master.

ANTONY
175 So is the fame.
Would we had spoke together! Haste we for it.
Yet, ere we put ourselves in arms, dispatch we
The business we have talked of.

CAESAR
                                        With most gladness,
And do invite you to my sister's view,
180 Whither straight I'll lead you.

ANTONY
Let us, Lepidus, not lack your company.

LEPIDUS
Noble Antony, not sickness should detain me.

Flourish. Exeunt all but ENOBARBUS, AGRIPPA,
and MAECENAS

MAECENAS
(to ENOBARBUS*)* Welcome from Egypt, sir.

ENOBARBUS
Half the heart of Caesar, worthy Maecenas! My honorable
185 friend, Agrippa.

AGRIPPA
Good Enobarbus!

MAECENAS
We have cause to be glad that matters are so well digested.
You stayed well by 't in Egypt.

ENOBARBUS
Ay, sir, we did sleep day out of countenance and made the
190 night light with drinking.

CAESAR

Large and increasing. But his navy rules the sea.

ANTONY

That's what I hear. I wish we'd had this conversation sooner. Let's get down to business—and yet, before we get ready for war, let's take care of that business we just discussed.

CAESAR

With pleasure. I'll introduce you to my sister. Follow me.

ANTONY

Come with us, Lepidus.

LEPIDUS

Noble Antony, even illness couldn't keep me away.

Trumpets play a fanfare. Everyone exits except ENOBARBUS, AGRIPPA, *and* MAECENAS.

MAECENAS

(to ENOBARBUS*)* Welcome back from Egypt, sir.

ENOBARBUS

You've become Caesar's right hand man, Maecenas! It's good to see you too, Agrippa.

AGRIPPA

Good Enobarbus!

MAECENAS

We can be happy that things have been resolved so agreeably. And I see you survived your time in Egypt.

ENOBARBUS

Yes, sir, it was tough. We confused the daytime by sleeping through it, and made the night merry with our drinking.

MAECENAS
Eight wild boars roasted whole at a breakfast—and but
twelve persons there! Is this true?

ENOBARBUS
This was but as a fly by an eagle. We had much more
monstrous matter of feast, which worthily deserved noting.

195 **MAECENAS**
She's a most triumphant lady, if report be square to her.

ENOBARBUS
When she first met Mark Antony, she pursed up his heart
upon the river of Cydnus.

AGRIPPA
There she appeared indeed, or my reporter devised well for
her.

ENOBARBUS
200 I will tell you.
The barge she sat in, like a burnished throne,
Burned on the water. The poop was beaten gold,
Purple the sails, and so perfumèd that
The winds were lovesick with them. The oars were silver,
205 Which to the tune of flutes kept stroke, and made
The water which they beat to follow faster,
As amorous of their strokes. For her own person,
It beggared all description: she did lie
In her pavilion—cloth-of-gold, of tissue—
210 O'erpicturing that Venus where we see
The fancy outwork nature. On each side her
Stood pretty dimpled boys, like smiling Cupids,
With divers-colored fans, whose wind did seem
To glow the delicate cheeks which they did cool,
215 And what they undid did.

AGRIPPA
                          Oh, rare for Antony!

MAECENAS

> We heard that once you were served eight wild boars roasted whole for breakfast—for only twelve people! Is that true?

ENOBARBUS

> That was nothing. There were many even more memorable feasts.

MAECENAS

> She's a remarkable lady, if the rumors are to be believed.

ENOBARBUS

River in southern Turkey

> From the first time Antony saw her, sailing on her barge on the Cydnus River, he was hers.

AGRIPPA

> She made quite an appearance there, or else my informant invented a very flattering description of her.

ENOBARBUS

> I'll tell you. Her barge looked like a golden throne upon the waves, burning bright with the sun's reflections. The rear deck was covered with hammered gold. The sails were dyed purple, and they were perfumed so heavily that they made the air seem dizzy with love. The oars were made of silver, and the oarsmen rowed in time to flute music. As the oars beat the water, the waves seemed to speed up as if excited by lust. Cleopatra's appearance was indescribable. As she reclined under a canopy woven from gold thread, she was more beautiful than any artist's idealized portrait of the goddess Venus. Pretty, Cupid-like boys stood on either side of her, smiling and cooling her with multicolored fans, which seemed to fan the flames in her cheeks even as they cooled them, undoing what they did.

AGRIPPA

> How excellent for Antony!

ENOBARBUS
　　　　Her gentlewomen, like the Nereides,
　　　　So many mermaids, tended her i' th' eyes,
　　　　And made their bends adornings. At the helm
　　　　A seeming mermaid steers. The silken tackle
220　　　Swell with the touches of those flower-soft hands
　　　　That yarely frame the office. From the barge
　　　　A strange invisible perfume hits the sense
　　　　Of the adjacent wharfs. The city cast
　　　　Her people out upon her, and Antony,
225　　　Enthroned i' th' marketplace, did sit alone,
　　　　Whistling to th' air, which, but for vacancy,
　　　　Had gone to gaze on Cleopatra too
　　　　And made a gap in nature.

AGRIPPA
　　　　　　　　　　　　　　　Rare Egyptian!

ENOBARBUS
　　　　Upon her landing, Antony sent to her,
230　　　Invited her to supper. She replied
　　　　It should be better he became her guest,
　　　　Which she entreated. Our courteous Antony,
　　　　Whom ne'er the word of "No" woman heard speak,
　　　　Being barbered ten times o'er, goes to the feast,
235　　　And for his ordinary pays his heart
　　　　For what his eyes eat only.

AGRIPPA
　　　　　　　　　　　　　Royal wench!
　　　　She made great Caesar lay his sword to bed.
　　　　He plowed her, and she cropped.

ENOBARBUS
　　　　　　　　　　　　　　I saw her once
　　　　Hop forty paces through the public street,
240　　　And having lost her breath, she spoke, and panted,
　　　　That she did make defect perfection,
　　　　And, breathless, pour breathe forth.

ENOBARBUS

Nereides = sea nymphs

Her ladies-in-waiting—like Nereides, or mermaids —tended to Cleopatra as she watched them, and their graceful movements added to the beauty of the scene. It seemed as if a mermaid were steering. The silken sails and ropes swelled in the wind, expertly handled by the ladies' soft hands. People on the wharves could smell exotic perfume wafting from the barge as it passed them. All the people came out to see her, and Antony, waiting for her in the marketplace, was left alone. Even the air itself would have gone to look at Cleopatra, if that wouldn't have caused an unnatural vacuum in the atmosphere.

AGRIPPA

Extraordinary Egyptian!

ENOBARBUS

When she landed at the port, Antony sent an invitation for her to come to supper. She replied by saying that it would be better for him to be her guest instead. Our courteous Antony, who has never said "no" to any woman, after spending plenty of time being groomed by the barber, goes to the feast. For that simple meal, he paid with his heart—even though it was only his eyes that were satisfied.

AGRIPPA

Their son, Caesarion

Royal seductress! She lured Julius Caesar into her bed, he made love to her, and she bore his child.

ENOBARBUS

I saw her once hop forty feet down the street. When she stopped she was so out of breath that she was panting. Her beauty made even that weakness seem perfect, and even in her breathlessness she seemed to pour out breath.

MAECENAS
  Now Antony must leave her utterly.

ENOBARBUS
  Never. He will not.
245 Age cannot wither her, nor custom stale
  Her infinite variety. Other women cloy
  The appetites they feed, but she makes hungry
  Where most she satisfies, for vilest things
  Become themselves in her, that the holy priests
250 Bless her when she is riggish.

MAECENAS
  If beauty, wisdom, modesty, can settle
  The heart of Antony, Octavia is
  A blessèd lottery to him.

AGRIPPA
                    Let us go.
  Good Enobarbus, make yourself my guest
255 Whilst you abide here.

ENOBARBUS
                    Humbly, sir, I thank you.
                                        Exeunt

MAECENAS

Now Antony has to leave her completely.

ENOBARBUS

He'll never leave her. Age won't wither her, and her charms are so varied that she never grows boring. With other women, the more familiar you grow with them the less appealing they become. Cleopatra, on the other hand, makes you desire her the more you see her. Even her worst faults are charming, and holy priests bless her even when she acts the slut.

MAECENAS

If beauty, wisdom, and modesty can settle Antony's restless heart, Octavia will be the best thing that has ever happened to him.

AGRIPPA

Let's go. Good Enobarbus, consider yourself my guest as long as you're here.

ENOBARBUS

I humbly thank you.

They exit.

ACT 2, SCENE 3

Enter ANTONY, CAESAR; OCTAVIA *between them*

ANTONY
    (to OCTAVIA*)* The world and my great office will sometimes
    Divide me from your bosom.

OCTAVIA
                            All which time
    Before the gods my knee shall bow my prayers
    To them for you.

ANTONY
            (to CAESAR*)*   Good night, sir.—My Octavia,
5   Read not my blemishes in the world's report.
    I have not kept my square, but that to come
    Shall all be done by th' rule. Good night, dear lady.
    (to CAESAR*)* Good night, sir.

CAESAR
    Good night.

                            He exits with OCTAVIA

    Enter SOOTHSAYER

ANTONY
10   Now, sirrah, you do wish yourself in Egypt?

SOOTHSAYER
    Would I had never come from thence, nor you thither.

ANTONY
    If you can, your reason?

SOOTHSAYER
    I see it in my motion, have it not in my tongue. But yet hie
    you to Egypt again.

ACT 2, SCENE 3

ANTONY and CAESAR enter with OCTAVIA between them.

ANTONY

(to OCTAVIA) There will be times when my duties and responsibilities take me away from you.

OCTAVIA

And I will spend our time apart on my knees, praying for you.

ANTONY

(to CAESAR) Good night, sir. My Octavia, don't believe everything you hear about me. I haven't always lived a conventional life, but the future will be by the book. Good night, dear lady. *(to CAESAR)* Good night, sir.

CAESAR

Good night.

CAESAR and OCTAVIA exit.

The FORTUNETELLER enters.

ANTONY

sirrah = term of address for a person of lower status

Now, sirrah, I hear you wish you were back in Egypt.

FORTUNETELLER

I wish I had never left Egypt and that you had never come to Egypt.

ANTONY

Tell me why, if you can.

FORTUNETELLER

It's a feeling, but nothing I can put into words. But you had better get back to Egypt again.

ANTONY

15   Say to me whose fortunes shall rise higher,
        Caesar's or mine?

SOOTHSAYER

        Caesar's.
        Therefore, O Antony, stay not by his side.
        Thy dæmon—that thy spirit which keeps thee—is
20   Noble, courageous, high, unmatchable
        Where Caesar's is not. But near him thy angel
        Becomes afeard, as being o'erpowered. Therefore
        Make space enough between you.

ANTONY

                                        Speak this no more.

SOOTHSAYER

        To none but thee, no more but when to thee.
25   If thou dost play with him at any game,
        Thou art sure to lose, and of that natural luck
        He beats thee 'gainst the odds. Thy luster thickens
        When he shines by. I say again, thy spirit
        Is all afraid to govern thee near him,
30   But, he away, 'tis noble.

ANTONY

                                  Get thee gone.
        Say to Ventidius I would speak with him.

                                        Exit **SOOTHSAYER**

        (to himself) He shall to Parthia. Be it art or hap,
        He hath spoken true. The very dice obey him,
        And in our sports my better cunning faints
35   Under his chance. If we draw lots, he speeds.
        His cocks do win the battle still of mine
        When it is all to naught, and his quails ever
        Beat mine, inhooped, at odds. I will to Egypt.
        And though I make this marriage for my peace,
40   I' th' East my pleasure lies.

ANTONY

Tell me who shall have the better luck, Caesar or me?

FORTUNETELLER

Caesar. So you'd better not stay with him, Antony. Your guardian angel is noble, courageous, significant, and unmatched when Caesar's not around. But when you are with him, your angel is weakened and easily frightened. That's why there must be space between you.

ANTONY

Don't speak of this again.

FORTUNETELLER

To none but you, only to you. You will surely lose any game you play with Caesar. With his natural luck, he will beat you even against the odds. Your light dulls when he is near. I repeat: your angel is afraid to inspire you when you're around him, but when he goes away it becomes brilliant again.

ANTONY

Leave now. Tell Ventidius I want to speak with him.
                              The FORTUNETELLER *exits.*

(to himself) I'll send him to Parthia. Whether he's truly gifted or just lucky, what the Fortuneteller said is true. Even the dice obey Caesar. When we compete in sports, my skill is defeated by his luck. If we pick numbers in a lottery, he wins. His roosters always beat mine at the cockfights. His quails beat mine, even against the odds, when mine have the advantage. I'll return to Egypt. Though I've made this marriage to keep peace with Caesar, my pleasure remains in the East, with Cleopatra.

Enter VENTIDIUS

                              O come, Ventidius.
You must to Parthia. Your commission's ready.
Follow me and receive 't.

                                                    Exeunt

VENTIDIUS *enters.*

Come here, Ventidius. You must go to Parthia. Your authorization is ready. Come with me and I'll get it for you.

They exit.

ACT 2, SCENE 4

Enter LEPIDUS, MECAENAS, *and* AGRIPPA

LEPIDUS
Trouble yourselves no further. Pray you, hasten
Your generals after.

AGRIPPA
                    Sir, Mark Antony
Will e'en but kiss Octavia, and we'll follow.

LEPIDUS
Till I shall see you in your soldiers' dress,
5   Which will become you both, farewell.

MAECENAS
                                    We shall,
As I conceive the journey, be at the Mount
Before you, Lepidus.

LEPIDUS
                    Your way is shorter.
My purposes do draw me much about.
You'll win two days upon me.

MAECENAS, AGRIPPA
                            Sir, good success.

LEPIDUS
10   Farewell.

                                        Exeunt

ACT 2, SCENE 4

LEPIDUS, MAECENAS, *and* AGRIPPA *enter.*

LEPIDUS

Don't spend any more time here. Go tell your generals to hurry their preparations.

AGRIPPA

Sir, we'll follow as soon as Mark Antony kisses Octavia good-bye.

LEPIDUS

Good-bye then, until the time I see you dressed in your battle gear, which will suit you both very well.

MAECENAS

According to my reckoning, we'll get to Mt. Misena before you, Lepidus.

LEPIDUS

You're taking a shorter route. My plans take me a roundabout way. You'll get there two days before me.

BOTH

Good luck, sir.

LEPIDUS

Farewell.

They exit.

ACT 2, SCENE 5

Enter CLEOPATRA, CHARMIAN, IRAS, *and* ALEXAS

CLEOPATRA
Give me some music. Music, moody food
Of us that trade in love.

ALL
The music, ho!

Enter MARDIAN *the eunuch*

CLEOPATRA
Let it alone. Let's to billiards. Come, Charmian.

CHARMIAN
My arm is sore. Best play with Mardian.

CLEOPATRA
5   As well a woman with an eunuch played
As with a woman.—Come, you'll play with me, sir?

MARDIAN
As well as I can, madam.

CLEOPATRA
And when good will is showed, though 't come too short,
The actor may plead pardon. I'll none now.
10 Give me mine angle. We'll to th' river. There,
My music playing far off, I will betray
Tawny-finned fishes. My bended hook shall pierce
Their slimy jaws, and as I draw them up
I'll think them every one an Antony
15 And say, "Aha! You're caught."

CHARMIAN
'Twas merry when
You wagered on your angling, when your diver
Did hang a salt fish on his hook, which he
With fervency drew up.

ACT 2, SCENE 5

CLEOPATRA, CHARMIAN, IRAS, *and* ALEXAS *enter.*

CLEOPATRA

Play me some music. Music feeds the melancholy moods of us lovers.

ALL

Musicians, come in!

MADRIAN *enters.*

CLEOPATRA

Never mind. Let's play billiards. Play with me, Charmian.

CHARMIAN

My arm is sore. You'll have a better game with Mardian.

CLEOPATRA

Playing with a eunuch is the same as playing with a woman. Will you play with me, sir?

MARDIAN

I'll do my best, madam.

CLEOPATRA

When a person tries in good faith, even if he fails he cannot be blamed. I don't want to play now. Give me my fishing rod. We'll go to the river. With my music playing in the background, I'll lure fish. My hook will go through their slimy jaws and as I pull them up I'll imagine each one is Antony. I'll say, "Aha! I caught you!"

CHARMIAN

It was funny when you and Antony bet on who could catch the first fish. You had a diver put a salted fish on his hook. He was so excited as he hurried to pull it in!

CLEOPATRA

That time—Oh, times!—
I laughed him out of patience, and that night
20   I laughed him into patience. And next morn,
Ere the ninth hour, I drunk him to his bed,
Then put my tires and mantles on him, whilst
I wore his sword Philippan.

Enter a MESSENGER

Oh, from Italy!
Ram thou thy fruitful tidings in mine ears,
25   That long time have been barren.

MESSENGER

Madam, madam—

CLEOPATRA

Antonio's dead! If thou say so, villain,
Thou kill'st thy mistress. But well and free,
If thou so yield him, there is gold, and here
My bluest veins to kiss—a hand that kings
30   Have lipped, and trembled kissing.

MESSENGER

First, madam, he is well.

CLEOPATRA

Why, there's more gold. But, sirrah, mark, we use
To say the dead are well. Bring it to that,
The gold I give thee will I melt and pour
35   Down thy ill-uttering throat.

MESSENGER

Good madam, hear me.

CLEOPATRA

Well, go to, I will.
But there's no goodness in thy face—if Antony
Be free and healthful, so tart a favor
40   To trumpet such good tidings! If not well,

CLEOPATRA

That time? Oh, there were so many fun times. I would play some trick on him and laugh until he lost his patience. Then, that night, I would laugh with him while we made love until he was patient again. Then by nine in the morning I would have him so drunk I could dress him in my clothes while I wore the sword he used at the famous battle of Philippi.

A **MESSENGER** *enters.*

Oh! News from Italy! Cram your good news into my ears. It's been so long since I've heard from him.

MESSENGER

Madam, madam—

CLEOPATRA

Antony's dead! If you say that, you bastard, you'll kill your Queen. If you say he's healthy and free, I'll give you money and you may kiss my hand. Kings have trembled to kiss this hand.

MESSENGER

Let me say first, madam, that he is well.

CLEOPATRA

Well then, here's more money for you. But you know, sirrah, we customarily say that the dead are well. If that's what you mean, I'll melt this gold and pour it down your throat that speaks these hateful words.

MESSENGER

Good madam, let me speak.

CLEOPATRA

All right, I will. But you don't look as if you bring good news. If Antony is free and healthy, you shouldn't wear such a sour face while bringing such good news.

Thou shouldst come like a Fury crowned with snakes,
Not like a formal man.

MESSENGER

Will 't please you hear me?

CLEOPATRA

I have a mind to strike thee ere thou speak'st.
Yet if thou say Antony lives, is well,
Or friends with Caesar, or not captive to him,
I'll set thee in a shower of gold and hail
Rich pearls upon thee.

MESSENGER

Madam, he's well.

CLEOPATRA

Well said.

MESSENGER

And friends with Caesar.

CLEOPATRA

Th' art an honest man.

MESSENGER

Caesar and he are greater friends than ever.

CLEOPATRA

Make thee a fortune from me.

MESSENGER

But yet, madam—

CLEOPATRA

I do not like "But yet." It does allay
The good precedence. Fie upon "But yet."
"But yet" is as a jailer to bring forth
Some monstrous malefactor. Prithee, friend,
Pour out the pack of matter to mine ear,
The good and bad together. He's friends with Caesar,
In state of health, thou say'st, and, thou say'st, free.

MESSENGER

Free, madam, no. I made no such report.
He's bound unto Octavia.

Furies = mythological figures who punished those who broke either natural or moral laws

If he's not well, you should arrive like a Fury with snakes for hair, not in the shape of a normal man.

MESSENGER

Do you want to hear my news?

CLEOPATRA

I have half a mind to hit you before you speak again. But if Antony is alive, healthy, friendly with Caesar, and not Caesar's prisoner, I'll shower you with gold and pearls.

MESSENGER

Madam, he's well.

CLEOPATRA

That's well spoken.

MESSENGER

And he's friendly with Caesar.

CLEOPATRA

You are an honest man.

MESSENGER

Caesar and he are better friends than ever.

CLEOPATRA

I'm going to make you a rich man.

MESSENGER

But yet, madam—

CLEOPATRA

I don't like the sound of "but yet." It reverses all the good that came before it. Damn those words, "but yet!" "But yet" is like a jailer about to bring out some horrible criminal. Please, my friend, give me all the news, both good and bad, at the same time. You say he's friendly with Caesar, healthy, and free.

MESSENGER

I didn't say free, madam. No, I didn't say that. He's bound to Octavia.

CLEOPATRA
                    For what good turn?

60 **MESSENGER**
    For the best turn i' th' bed.

CLEOPATRA
                        I am pale, Charmian.

MESSENGER
    Madam, he's married to Octavia.

CLEOPATRA
    The most infectious pestilence upon thee!

Strikes him down

MESSENGER
    Good madam, patience.

CLEOPATRA
    What say you?

Strikes him

65   Hence, horrible villain, or I'll spurn thine eyes
    Like balls before me! I'll unhair thy head!

She hales him up and down

    Thou shalt be whipped with wire and stewed in brine,
    Smarting in ling'ring pickle!

MESSENGER
                        Gracious madam,
    I that do bring the news made not the match.

CLEOPATRA
70   Say 'tis not so, a province I will give thee
    And make thy fortunes proud. The blow thou hadst
    Shall make thy peace for moving me to rage,
    And I will boot thee with what gift beside
    Thy modesty can beg.

CLEOPATRA

For what favor?

MESSENGER

For the favor of sleeping in her bed.

CLEOPATRA

I'm sick, Charmian.

MESSENGER

He's married to Octavia, madam.

CLEOPATRA

May you die of the worst disease!

She knocks him down.

MESSENGER

Good madam, be patient.

CLEOPATRA

What did you say to me?

She hits him again.

Get out, you horrible bastard, or I'll gouge out your eyes. I'll scalp you.

She drags him across the stage.

I'll have you whipped with wire and soaked in brine like a pickle, making your pain linger.

MESSENGER

Gracious madam, I only brought the news. I didn't make the match.

CLEOPATRA

If you say it isn't true, I'll give you a province and make you rich. The blows I gave you already will make up for your upsetting me. And on top of that I'll give you whatever you ask for.

MESSENGER
                              He's married, madam.

CLEOPATRA
75   Rogue, thou hast lived too long.

Draws a knife

MESSENGER
                                        Nay then, I'll run.
      What mean you, madam? I have made no fault.

                                                        Exit

CHARMIAN
      Good madam, keep yourself within yourself.
      The man is innocent.

CLEOPATRA
      Some innocents 'scape not the thunderbolt.
80   Melt Egypt into Nile, and kindly creatures
      Turn all to serpents. Call the slave again.
      Though I am mad, I will not bite him. Call!

CHARMIAN
      He is afeard to come.

CLEOPATRA
                              I will not hurt him.
      These hands do lack nobility that they strike
85   A meaner than myself, since I myself
      Have given myself the cause.

Enter the **MESSENGER** *again*

                                        Come hither, sir.
      Though it be honest, it is never good
      To bring bad news. Give to a gracious message
      An host of tongues, but let ill tidings tell
90   Themselves when they be felt.

MESSENGER
      I have done my duty.

MESSENGER

He's married, madam.

CLEOPATRA

Rogue, you've lived too long!

She draws a knife.

MESSENGER

No way, then, I'll run. What's the matter with you, madam? I haven't done anything to you.

The **MESSENGER** *exits.*

CHARMIAN

Good madam, restrain yourself. The man hasn't done anything wrong.

CLEOPATRA

Even innocents cannot always escape disaster. May Egypt drown in the Nile and all good creatures turn into poisonous snakes. Call that servant back. Even though I'm mad, I won't bite him. Call him!

CHARMIAN

He's afraid to come in.

CLEOPATRA

I won't hurt him. My hands are tainted if they hit an inferior, especially since I myself am the cause of my own distress.

The **MESSENGER** *returns.*

Come here, sir. It may be honest, but it's never wise to bring bad news. You can give good news in many ways, but let bad news interpret itself as you tell it.

MESSENGER

I've only done my duty.

CLEOPATRA
Is he married?
I cannot hate thee worser than I do
If thou again say "yes."

MESSENGER
                                          He's married, madam.

CLEOPATRA
95   The gods confound thee! Dost thou hold there still?

MESSENGER
Should I lie, madam?

CLEOPATRA
                              Oh, I would thou didst,
So half my Egypt were submerged and made
A cistern for scaled snakes! Go, get thee hence.
Hadst thou Narcissus in thy face, to me
100   Thou wouldst appear most ugly. He is married?

MESSENGER
I crave your highness' pardon.

CLEOPATRA
                                        He is married?

MESSENGER
Take no offense that I would not offend you.
To punish me for what you make me do
Seems much unequal. He's married to Octavia.

CLEOPATRA
105   Oh, that his fault should make a knave of thee,
That art not what th' art sure of! Get thee hence.
The merchandise which thou hast brought from Rome
Are all too dear for me. Lie they upon thy hand
And be undone by 'em!

                                        Exit MESSENGER

CHARMIAN
                              Good your highness, patience.

CLEOPATRA

> Is he married? I can't hate you any more than I already
> do if you repeat that he is.

MESSENGER

> He's married, madam.

CLEOPATRA

> May the gods destroy you! Do you maintain the same
> story?

MESSENGER

> Do you want me to lie, madam?

CLEOPATRA

> Oh, I wish you had lied, even if it meant half my king-
> dom would be submerged and filled with snakes. Go,
> get out! Even if you were as handsome as Narcissus,
> your face would be ugly to me. Is he really married?

*Narcissus =
mythical boy who
was so beautiful
that he drowned
himself while
trying to embrace
his own reflection*

MESSENGER

> I beg your highness' pardon.

CLEOPATRA

> Is he really married?

MESSENGER

> Please don't be offended that I don't want to offend
> you any more. It's not fair to punish me for something
> you make me do. He's married to Octavia.

CLEOPATRA

> It's too bad that Antony's fault should make you look
> like a jerk. You didn't have anything to do with it. Go
> away. The merchandise you bring from Rome is too
> expensive for me. Let it stay in your inventory until it
> bankrupts you.

> *The* **MESSENGER** *exits.*

CHARMIAN

> Be patient, your highness.

CLEOPATRA
110   In praising Antony, I have dispraised Caesar.

CHARMIAN
Many times, madam.

CLEOPATRA
I am paid for 't now. Lead me from hence.
I faint. O Iras, Charmian! 'Tis no matter.—
Go to the fellow, good Alexas. Bid him
115   Report the feature of Octavia: her years,
Her inclination. Let him not leave out
The color of her hair. Bring me word quickly.

Exit ALEXAS

Let him forever go!—Let him not, Charmian.
Though he be painted one way like a Gorgon,
120   The other way's a Mars. *(to* MARDIAN*)* Bid you Alexas
Bring me word how tall she is. Pity me, Charmian,
But do not speak to me. Lead me to my chamber.

Exeunt

CLEOPATRA

When I have praised Antony, I've disparaged Caesar.

CHARMIAN

Many times, madam.

CLEOPATRA

I'm being repaid for that now. Help me out of here. I feel faint. Oh, Iras, Charmian! It doesn't matter. Good Alexas, go ask that fellow to describe Octavia. How old is she? What kind of disposition does she have? Don't let him leave out the color of her hair. Bring me his answers quickly.

ALEXAS exits.

Let Antony be purged from my life forever—but no, don't let him, Charmian. Even though half of him is like a Gorgon, the other half is like Mars. *(to MARDIAN)* Ask Alexas to also ask him how tall she is. Feel sorry for me, Charmian, but don't talk to me. Help me get to my bedroom.

They exit.

Gorgons = mythical monsters whose gaze turned humans to stone

ACT 2, SCENE 6

Flourish. Enter POMPEY *and* MENAS *at one door, with drum and trumpet; at another* CAESAR, LEPIDUS, ANTONY, ENOBARBUS, MAECENAS, *and* AGRIPPA, *with soldiers marching*

POMPEY
Your hostages I have, so have you mine,
And we shall talk before we fight.

CAESAR
                                        Most meet
That first we come to words, and therefore have we
Our written purposes before us sent,
5   Which, if thou hast considered, let us know
If 'twill tie up thy discontented sword
And carry back to Sicily much tall youth
That else must perish here.

POMPEY
                                        To you all three,
The senators alone of this great world,
10   Chief factors for the gods: I do not know
Wherefore my father should revengers want,
Having a son and friends, since Julius Caesar,
Who at Philippi the good Brutus ghosted,
There saw you laboring for him. What was 't
15   That moved pale Cassius to conspire? And what
Made the all-honored, honest Roman Brutus,
With the armed rest, courtiers of beauteous freedom,
To drench the Capitol, but that they would
Have one man but a man? And that is it

ACT 2, SCENE 6

A trumpet fanfare sounds. POMPEY *and* MENAS *enter through one stage door to the music of a drum and a trumpet.* CAESAR, LEPIDUS, ANTONY, ENOBARBUS, MAECENAS, *and* AGRIPPA *enter through another door, followed by soldiers.*

POMPEY

In order to conduct negotiations in safety, warring sides exchanged important persons and held the hostages until negotiations were complete.

I have your hostages and you have mine. Let's talk before we fight.

CAESAR

It's proper that we speak first, which is why we sent our proposals ahead of us for your consideration. If you've had time to think over these points, let us know whether they will relieve your frustration. If yes, then a lot of brave young men can return to Sicily who would otherwise die here.

POMPEY

I address the three of you, the sole rulers of this world and the main arbiters of the gods' will. I don't know why my father's death shouldn't be avenged, since he has a son and friends to do it. You avenged Julius Caesar's death at Philippi, where his ghost haunted his killer, Brutus. Why did Cassius conspire against Caesar? And why did the honorable, well-intentioned Brutus and the others, men devoted to the ideal of freedom, assassinate Caesar? They didn't want one man to be king in Rome.

20   Hath made me rig my navy, at whose burden
The angered ocean foams, with which I meant
To scourge th' ingratitude that despiteful Rome
Cast on my noble father.

CAESAR
                                        Take your time.

ANTONY
Thou canst not fear us, Pompey, with thy sails.
25   We'll speak with thee at sea. At land, thou know'st
How much we do o'ercount thee.

POMPEY
                                        At land indeed
Thou dost o'ercount me of my father's house,
But since the cuckoo builds not for himself,
Remain in 't as thou mayst.

LEPIDUS
                                  Be pleased to tell us—
30   For this is from the present—how you take
The offers we have sent you.

CAESAR
                                        There's the point.

ANTONY
Which do not be entreated to, but weigh
What it is worth embraced.

CAESAR
                                  And what may follow,
To try a larger fortune.

POMPEY
                            You have made me offer
35   Of Sicily, Sardinia. And I must
Rid all the sea of pirates, then, to send
Measures of wheat to Rome. This 'greed upon
To part with unhacked edges and bear back
Our targes undinted.

CAESAR, ANTONY, LEPIDUS
                                  That's our offer.

And that's why I've built my navy, which is so huge that the weight of the ships makes the sea foam with anger. I will punish Rome for her ingratitude toward my noble father.

CAESAR

Take your time.

ANTONY

Pompey, you cannot frighten us with your navy. We'll meet you at sea. You know that on land our army is far greater than yours.

POMPEY

Cuckoo birds lay their eggs in other birds' nests.

Yes, on land you do outnumber me. Even more since you annexed my father's house and lands. But since, like the cuckoo, you don't build anything for yourself, live in those lands as long as you can.

LEPIDUS

To get back to the matter at hand, what do you think of our proposal?

CAESAR

That's the point.

ANTONY

Don't let us talk you into anything, but consider carefully the value of our offers.

CAESAR

And consider the possible consequences of fighting against us, in the hopes of gaining a greater fortune.

POMPEY

You have offered me the lands of Sicily and Sardinia. In return, I must clear the sea of pirates and send tributes of wheat to Rome. If I agree to this, we may leave unharmed, with our shields undented.

CAESAR, ANTONY, *and* **LEPIDUS**
That's our offer.

POMPEY
                                                    Know then
40   I came before you here a man prepared
      To take this offer, but Mark Antony
      Put me to some impatience. *(to* ANTONY*)*—Though I lose
      The praise of it by telling, you must know,
      When Caesar and your brother were at blows,
45   Your mother came to Sicily and did find
      Her welcome friendly.

ANTONY
                (to POMPEY*)*   I have heard it, Pompey,
      And am well studied for a liberal thanks
      Which I do owe you.

POMPEY
                                    Let me have your hand.

      They clasp hands

      I did not think, sir, to have met you here.

ANTONY
50   The beds i' th' East are soft, and thanks to you,
      That called me timelier than my purpose hither,
      For I have gained by 't.

CAESAR
                (to POMPEY*)*   Since I saw you last
      There's a change upon you.

POMPEY
                                        Well, I know not
      What counts harsh Fortune casts upon my face,
55   But in my bosom shall she never come
      To make my heart her vassal.

LEPIDUS
                                        Well met here.

POMPEY

You should know that when I came here I was prepared to accept your offer. But Mark Antony made me somewhat angry. *(to* ANTONY*)* Though it would be nobler to for me not to speak of this good act myself, you should know that when Caesar and your brother were fighting, your mother came to Sicily for refuge. I welcomed her gladly.

ANTONY

(to POMPEY*)* I heard what you did for her, Pompey, and want to give you the many thanks I owe you.

POMPEY

Let me shake your hand.

They shake hands.

I didn't think I would see you here.

ANTONY

The East is very seductive. I have you to thank for my trip here; I wouldn't have left Egypt otherwise, and I have benefited from it.

CAESAR

(to POMPEY*)* You've changed since the last time I saw you.

POMPEY

Well, I cannot tell how my difficult life has weathered my face, but I will never let those difficulties subdue my courage.

LEPIDUS

It's good we had this meeting.

POMPEY
I hope so, Lepidus. Thus we are agreed.
I crave our composition may be written
And sealed between us.

CAESAR
                         That's the next to do.

POMPEY
60   We'll feast each other ere we part, and let's
Draw lots who shall begin.

ANTONY
                              That will I, Pompey.

POMPEY
No, Antony, take the lot. But, first or last,
Your fine Egyptian cookery shall have
The fame. I have heard that Julius Caesar
65   Grew fat with feasting there.

ANTONY
You have heard much.

POMPEY
I have fair meanings, sir.

ANTONY
And fair words to them.

POMPEY
Then so much have I heard.
70   And I have heard Apollodorus carried—

ENOBARBUS
(interrupting POMPEY*)* No more of that. He did so.

POMPEY
                                   What, I pray you?

ENOBARBUS
A certain queen to Caesar in a mattress.

POMPEY

I hope it works out for the best, Lepidus. So we are in agreement. Please have the contract written up so we can all sign it.

CAESAR

That's the next thing on the agenda.

POMPEY

We'll have celebration feasts for each other before we go our separate ways. Let's draw lots to see who will host the first one.

ANTONY

I'll give the first one, Pompey.

POMPEY

No, Antony. Pick one of these lots. Whether your banquet is first or last, your Egyptian cooking will make it the best. I heard that Julius Caesar got fat from all the feasting there.

ANTONY

You've heard a lot.

POMPEY

I mean well, sir.

ANTONY

I'm sure you do.

POMPEY

I've heard a lot more. I heard that Apollodorus carried—

ENOBARBUS

(interrupting POMPEY) That's enough of that. Yes, it's true.

POMPEY

What did he carry, please?

ENOBARBUS

A certain queen to Caesar, rolled up in a mattress.

According to Plutarch, this is how Cleopatra managed to secretly tryst with Julius Caesar.

POMPEY
    I know thee now. How far'st thou, soldier?

ENOBARBUS
                                           Well,
    And well am like to do, for I perceive,
75   Four feasts are toward.

POMPEY
                     Let me shake thy hand.
    I never hated thee. I have seen thee fight
    When I have envied thy behavior.

ENOBARBUS
                                   Sir,
    I never loved you much, but I ha' praised ye
    When you have well deserved ten times as much
80   As I have said you did.

POMPEY
                    Enjoy thy plainness.
    It nothing ill becomes thee.—
    Aboard my galley I invite you all.
    Will you lead, lords?

CAESAR, ANTONY, LEPIDUS
                  Show 's the way, sir.

POMPEY
                              Come.
                Exeunt all but ENOBARBUS *and* MENAS

MENAS
    (aside) Thy father, Pompey, would ne'er have made this
85   treaty. *(to* ENOBARBUS*)* You and I have known, sir.

ENOBARBUS
    At sea, I think.

MENAS
    We have, sir.

ENOBARBUS
    You have done well by water.

POMPEY

> Now I know who you are. How are you, soldier?

ENOBARBUS

> I'm well, and probably will be for a while, as I hear that four feasts are being prepared.

POMPEY

> Let me shake your hand. I've never been your enemy. I've seen you fight and envied your skill.

ENOBARBUS

> Sir, I wouldn't say I was your friend, but I've praised you when you deserved ten times more praise than I gave.

POMPEY

> Enjoy your frankness; it suits you. I invite you all aboard my ship. After you, my lords?

CAESAR, ANTONY, AND LEPIDUS

> Show us the way, sir.

POMPEY

> Come with me.
> > *Everyone exits except for* ENOBARBUS *and* MENAS.

MENAS

> *(to himself)* Your father would never have agreed to this treaty, Pompey. *(to* ENOBARBUS*)* You and I have met, sir.

ENOBARBUS

> I think it was at sea.

MENAS

> That it was, sir.

ENOBARBUS

> You've done well at sea.

MENAS
> And you by land.

ENOBARBUS
90
> I will praise any man that will praise me, though it cannot
> be denied what I have done by land.

MENAS
> Nor what I have done by water.

ENOBARBUS
> Yes, something you can deny for your own safety: you have
> been a great thief by sea.

MENAS
95
> And you by land.

ENOBARBUS
> There I deny my land service. But give me your hand,
> Menas.

They clasp hands

> If our eyes had authority, here they might take two thieves
> kissing.

MENAS
100
> All men's faces are true, whatsome'er their hands are.

ENOBARBUS
> But there is never a fair woman has a true face.

MENAS
> No slander. They steal hearts.

ENOBARBUS
> We came hither to fight with you.

MENAS
> For my part, I am sorry it is turned to a drinking. Pompey
105
> doth this day laugh away his fortune.

ENOBARBUS
> If he do, sure he cannot weep 't back again.

MENAS
> You've said, sir. We looked not for Mark Antony here. Pray
> you, is he married to Cleopatra?

MENAS

And you've done well on land.

ENOBARBUS

I'll flatter anyone who flatters me—though what I've accomplished on land cannot be denied.

MENAS

Neither can my accomplishments at sea.

ENOBARBUS

Yes, for your own safety, you should deny one thing: you have been a great thief at sea.

MENAS

As you were on land.

ENOBARBUS

That's the one part of my service on land I do deny. But let's shake hands, Menas.

They shake.

If our eyes were policemen, they might capture two thieves at once while we're embracing.

MENAS

Men's faces are truthful, whatever their hands do.

ENOBARBUS

But no beautiful woman has an honest face.

MENAS

That's no lie. They steal hearts.

ENOBARBUS

We came here to fight against you.

MENAS

For my part, I'm sorry this battle turned into a drinking match. Today Pompey laughs away his fortune.

ENOBARBUS

If that's true, he won't get it back by crying.

MENAS

That's the truth, sir. We didn't expect Mark Antony to be here. Is he married to Cleopatra?

ENOBARBUS
Caesar's sister is called Octavia.

MENAS
110   True, sir. She was the wife of Caius Marcellus.

ENOBARBUS
But she is now the wife of Marcus Antonius.

MENAS
Pray ye, sir?

ENOBARBUS
'Tis true.

MENAS
Then is Caesar and he forever knit together.

ENOBARBUS
115   If I were bound to divine of this unity, I would not prophesy
so.

MENAS
I think the policy of that purpose made more in the
marriage than the love of the parties.

ENOBARBUS
I think so too. But you shall find the band that seems to tie
120   their friendship together will be the very strangler of their
amity. Octavia is of a holy, cold, and still conversation.

MENAS
Who would not have his wife so?

ENOBARBUS
Not he that himself is not so, which is Mark Antony. He
will to his Egyptian dish again. Then shall the sighs of
125   Octavia blow the fire up in Caesar, and, as I said before, that
which is the strength of their amity shall prove the
immediate author of their variance. Antony will use his
affection where it is. He married but his occasion here.

MENAS
And thus it may be. Come, sir, will you aboard? I have a
130   health for you.

ENOBARBUS

Caesar's sister is named Octavia.

MENAS

That's true, sir. She was previously Caius Marcellus' wife.

ENOBARBUS

But she is now Mark Antony's wife.

MENAS

Excuse me, sir?

ENOBARBUS

It's true.

MENAS

Then Caesar and he will always be united.

ENOBARBUS

If I were to make a prediction regarding this union, I wouldn't say that.

MENAS

I think the marriage was made more for political reasons than for love.

ENOBARBUS

I think so too. But you'll see that the very thing that joins them will be the thing that separates them. Octavia has a pious, chaste, meek disposition.

MENAS

Doesn't everyone want a wife like that?

ENOBARBUS

Not someone who doesn't share that disposition, meaning Mark Antony. He'll go back to his Egyptian dish. Then Octavia's complaints will rouse Caesar, and as I said before, the thing that brought them together will part them. Antony will go where his passion is. He only married out of political necessity.

MENAS

Then that's the way it may turn out. Come on, sir, will you come aboard? I want to drink your health.

ENOBARBUS
    I shall take it, sir. We have used our throats in Egypt.

MENAS
    Come, let's away.

Exeunt

ENOBARBUS

I'll join you, sir. We did a lot of drinking in Egypt.

MENAS

Let's go.

They exit.

ACT 2, SCENE 7

Music plays. Enter two or three SERVANTS *with a banquet*

FIRST SERVANT
Here they'll be, man. Some o' their plants are ill-rooted
already. The least wind i' th' world will blow them down.

SECOND SERVANT
Lepidus is high-colored.

FIRST SERVANT
They have made him drink alms-drink.

SECOND SERVANT
5   As they pinch one another by the disposition, he cries out,
"No more," reconciles them to his entreaty and himself to
th' drink.

FIRST SERVANT
But it raises the greater war between him and his discretion.

SECOND SERVANT
Why, this it is to have a name in great men's fellowship. I
10   had as lief have a reed that will do me no service as a partisan
I could not heave.

FIRST SERVANT
To be called into a huge sphere, and not to be seen to move
in 't, are the holes where eyes should be, which pitifully
disaster the cheeks.

A sennet sounded. Enter CAESAR, ANTONY, POMPEY,
LEPIDUS, AGRIPPA, MAECENAS, ENOBARBUS, *and* MENAS,
with other captains and a BOY

ANTONY
15   Thus do they, sir: they take the flow o' th' Nile
By certain scales i' th' Pyramid. They know
By th' height, the lowness, or the mean, if dearth

ACT 2, SCENE 7

Music plays. Two or three SERVANTS *enter with a feast.*

FIRST SERVANT

Here's where they'll end up, on the floor. Some of them are leaning already. It won't take much for them to fall over.

SECOND SERVANT

Lepidus is red in the face.

FIRST SERVANT

They made him drink the leftover wine usually given to the poor.

SECOND SERVANT

Their various personalities grate on one another. Lepidus cries, "No more arguing!" and then when they agree he resigns himself to drink.

FIRST SERVANT

Which goes on to impede his judgment.

SECOND SERVANT

That's what happens when you partner with great men but lack their power. I'd rather carry a reed that obviously can't protect me than a sword I cannot lift.

FIRST SERVANT

To be so unimportant in the company of important men is like having a face without any eyes.

A trumpet call sounds. CAESAR, ANTONY, POMPEY, LEPIDUS, AGRIPPA, MAECENAS, ENOBARBUS, *and* MENAS *enter, along with other captains and a* BOY.

ANTONY

This is how they do it, sir: they measure the depth of the Nile, according to certain marks made on the walls of the Pyramid. They know by those measurements if

Or foison follow. The higher Nilus swells
The more it promises. As it ebbs, the seedsman
20 Upon the slime and ooze scatters his grain,
And shortly comes to harvest.

LEPIDUS
You've strange serpents there?

ANTONY
Ay, Lepidus.

LEPIDUS
Your serpent of Egypt is bred now of your mud by the
25 operation of your sun. So is your crocodile.

ANTONY
They are so.

POMPEY
(to LEPIDUS*)* Sit, and some wine. A health to Lepidus!

They sit and drink

LEPIDUS
I am not so well as I should be, but I'll ne'er out.

ENOBARBUS
Not till you have slept. I fear me you'll be in till then.

LEPIDUS
30 Nay, certainly, I have heard the Ptolemies' pyramises are
very goodly things. Without contradiction I have heard
that.

MENAS
(aside to POMPEY*)* Pompey, a word.

POMPEY
(aside to MENAS*)* Say in mine ear. What is 't?

MENAS
35 *(aside to* POMPEY*)* Forsake thy seat, I do beseech thee,
                                 captain,
And hear me speak a word.

there will be famine or plenty. The higher the Nile flows, the better the harvest. As the river ebbs, the farmer scatters his seeds on the remaining silt. The harvest comes shortly after that.

LEPIDUS

Do you have unusual snakes there?

ANTONY

Yes, Lepidus.

LEPIDUS

The Egyptian snake is born when the sun shines on the Nile mud, just like the crocodile.

ANTONY

Yes, Lepidus.

POMPEY

Let's have a seat and some wine. A toast to Lepidus!

They sit and drink.

LEPIDUS

I don't feel so well, but I won't stop.

ENOBARBUS

Not until you pass out. I'm afraid you'll keep going until then.

LEPIDUS

No, I certainly won't stop. I've heard that the pyramids build by the Ptolemies are splendid. Without doubt I've heard that.

MENAS

(aside to POMPEY*)* Pompey, could I have a word with you?

POMPEY

(aside to MENAS*)* Whisper it in my ear. What is it?

MENAS

(whispers in POMPEY*'s ear)* Please, captain, leave the feast and let me speak with you privately.

POMPEY
> *(aside to* MENAS*)* Forbear me till anon.—This wine for
> Lepidus!

LEPIDUS
> What manner o' thing is your crocodile?

ANTONY
40
> It is shaped, sir, like itself, and it is as broad as it hath
> breadth. It is just so high as it is, and moves with its own
> organs. It lives by that which nourisheth it, and, the
> elements once out of it, it transmigrates.

LEPIDUS
> What color is it of?

ANTONY
> Of it own color too.

LEPIDUS
45
> 'Tis a strange serpent.

ANTONY
> 'Tis so. And the tears of it are wet.

CAESAR
> *(aside to* ANTONY*)* Will this description satisfy him?

ANTONY
> *(aside to* CAESAR*)* With the health that Pompey gives him,
> else he is a very epicure.

MENAS *whispers again*

POMPEY
50
> *(aside to* MENAS*)* Go hang, sir, hang! Tell me of that? Away!
> Do as I bid you.—Where's this cup I called for?

MENAS
> *(aside to* POMPEY*)* If for the sake of merit thou wilt hear me,
> Rise from thy stool.

POMPEY
> *(aside to* MENAS*)*   I think th' art mad.

POMPEY

(*aside to* MENAS) Leave me alone awhile. Where's the wine for Lepidus?

LEPIDUS

What does a crocodile look like?

ANTONY

Sir, it's shaped like itself and is as wide as it has width. It is only as high as it is and moves with its own legs. It lives on what nourishes it, and when the four elements leave it, its soul moves into another body.

the four elements =
fire, air, earth, and
water, thought to
be the building
blocks of all life

LEPIDUS

What color is it?

ANTONY

Its own color.

LEPIDUS

It's a strange snake.

ANTONY

It is that. And its tears are wet.

CAESAR

(*aside to* ANTONY) Will that description satisfy him?

ANTONY

(*aside to* CAESAR) That last toast Pompey gave him will take care of him, unless he's a raging glutton.

MENAS *whispers to* POMPEY *again.*

POMPEY

(*aside to* MENAS) Go to hell, sir. Are you still here? Go away! Do what I tell you. Where's the wine I ordered?

MENAS

(*aside to* POMPEY) If any service I've done you deserves a favor, get up from your stool and speak with me.

POMPEY

(*aside to* MENAS) I think you're crazy!

He rises, and they walk aside

                                        The matter?

MENAS
    I have ever held my cap off to thy fortunes.

POMPEY
55 Thou hast served me with much faith. What's else to say?—
    (to the others) Be jolly, lords.

ANTONY
                            These quicksands, Lepidus,
    Keep off them, for you sink.

MENAS
    (aside to POMPEY*)* Wilt thou be lord of all the world?

POMPEY
                                        What sayst thou?

MENAS
    Wilt thou be lord of the whole world? That's twice.

POMPEY
60 How should that be?

MENAS
    But entertain it,
    And, though thou think me poor, I am the man
    Will give thee all the world.

POMPEY
                            Hast thou drunk well?

MENAS
    No, Pompey, I have kept me from the cup.
65 Thou art, if thou dar'st be, the earthly Jove.
    Whate'er the ocean pales or sky inclips
    Is thine, if thou wilt ha 't.

POMPEY
                            Show me which way.

He gets up and walks aside with MENAS.

What is it?

MENAS

I've always had great respect for your destiny.

POMPEY

You've served me faithfully. What else can I say? *(to the others)* Be happy, lords!

ANTONY

Stay away from the quicksand of drink, Lepidus: you're sinking.

MENAS

(to POMPEY*)* Would you like to be king of the entire world?

POMPEY

What are you saying?

MENAS

Would you like to be king of the entire world? Now I've said it twice.

POMPEY

How could that happen?

MENAS

Just consider it. Though I seem poor, I am the man who will give you the world.

POMPEY

Are you drunk?

MENAS

No, Pompey, I haven't had anything to drink. You can be the most powerful man on earth if you dare use your power. Both land and sea are yours if you will take them.

POMPEY

Tell me how.

MENAS

These three world-sharers, these competitors,
Are in thy vessel. Let me cut the cable,
70 And, when we are put off, fall to their throats.
All there is thine.

POMPEY

                              Ah, this thou shouldst have done
And not have spoke on 't! In me 'tis villainy,
In thee 't had been good service. Thou must know,
'Tis not my profit that does lead mine honor;
75 Mine honor, it. Repent that e'er thy tongue
Hath so betrayed thine act. Being done unknown,
I should have found it afterwards well done,
But must condemn it now. Desist, and drink.

He returns to the feast

MENAS

(aside) For this,
80 I'll never follow thy palled fortunes more.
Who seeks and will not take when once 'tis offered
Shall never find it more.

POMPEY

                              This health to Lepidus!

ANTONY

(to a servant) Bear him ashore.—I'll pledge it for him,
          Pompey.

ENOBARBUS

Here's to thee, Menas!

They drink

MENAS

                              Enobarbus, welcome.

POMPEY

85 Fill till the cup be hid.

MENAS

The three who share the known world are aboard your boat. Let me cut the anchor cable. When we are away from land, cut their throats. Everything that belongs to them is yours.

POMPEY

Oh, you should have done it without telling me! For me to do such a thing would be dishonorable. For you to do it would be good service. You should know that to me, profit isn't more important than honor, but the other way around. Regret that your mouth betrayed your actions. If you had acted without my knowledge, I would have approved your action later. But now I must condemn it. Give it up and go drink.

He returns to the feast.

MENAS

(to himself) For this, I'll never be faithful to your declining fortunes again. A person who wants something but won't take it when it materializes won't get the opportunity again.

POMPEY

This toast is for Lepidus!

ANTONY

(to a servant) Help Lepidus ashore . . . I'll accept it for him, Pompey.

ENOBARBUS

Here's to you, Menas.

They drink.

MENAS

I accept with thanks, Enobarbus.

POMPEY

Fill the cups until they run over.

ENOBARBUS
There's a strong fellow, Menas.

Pointing to the servant who carries off LEPIDUS

MENAS
                                        Why?

ENOBARBUS
                                                He bears
The third part of the world, man. Seest not?

MENAS
The third part, then, is drunk. Would it were all,
That it might go on wheels!

ENOBARBUS
90   Drink thou. Increase the reels.

MENAS
Come.

POMPEY
This is not yet an Alexandrian feast.

ANTONY
It ripens towards it. Strike the vessels, ho!
Here's to Caesar.

CAESAR
                        I could well forbear 't.
95   It's monstrous labor when I wash my brain
And it grows fouler.

ANTONY
                        Be a child o' th' time.

CAESAR
Possess it, I'll make answer.
But I had rather fast from all four days
Than drink so much in one.

ENOBARBUS
            (to ANTONY*)*   Ha! My brave emperor,
100   Shall we dance now the Egyptian bacchanals
And celebrate our drink?

ENOBARBUS

There goes a strong fellow, Menas.

He points to the servant carrying LEPIDUS *away.*

MENAS

Why do you say that?

ENOBARBUS

He carries a third of the world. Can't you see that?

MENAS

Then a third of the world is drunk. I wish it were all drunk. Then everything would go more smoothly.

ENOBARBUS

Drink up. Liven up the party.

MENAS

All right, then.

POMPEY

This hasn't reached the level of an Egyptian feast yet.

ANTONY

It's getting there. Clink your cups together in a toast! Here's to Caesar.

CAESAR

I could do without another toast. It's unnatural. I keep washing my brain with alcohol, and it keeps getting fouler and more muddled.

ANTONY

Live in the moment.

CAESAR

I'd prefer to seize the day. But I would rather abstain from everything for four days than drink so much in one.

ENOBARBUS

bacchanals = bawdy dances honoring Bacchus, Roman god of wine

(to ANTONY*)* Ha! Shall we dance Egyptian bacchanals, my noble emperor, and celebrate our wine?

POMPEY
Let's ha 't, good soldier.

ANTONY
Come, let's all take hands
Till that the conquering wine hath steeped our sense
In soft and delicate Lethe.

ENOBARBUS
All take hands.
Make battery to our ears with the loud music,
The while I'll place you; then the boy shall sing.
The holding every man shall beat as loud
As his strong sides can volley.

Music plays. ENOBARBUS *places them hand in hand*

The Song.

BOY
(Sings)   Come, thou monarch of the vine,
            Plumpy Bacchus with pink eyne!
            In thy vats our cares be drowned,
            With thy grapes our hairs be crowned.

ALL
(Singing) Cup us till the world go round,
            Cup us till the world go round!

CAESAR
What would you more?—Pompey, good night. *(to* ANTONY*)*
Good brother,
Let me request you off. Our graver business
Frowns at this levity.—Gentle lords, let's part.
You see we have burnt our cheeks. Strong Enobarb
Is weaker than the wine; and mine own tongue
Splits what it speaks. The wild disguise hath almost
Anticked us all. What needs more words? Good night.
Good Antony, your hand.

POMPEY
I'll try you on the shore.

POMPEY

Let's have one, good soldier.

ANTONY

Come, let's join our hands until the overpowering wine makes us soft and forgetful.

ENOBARBUS

Everyone join hands. Attack our ears with loud music, and I'll position you for the dance. Then the boy will sing, and every man will sing the chorus at the top of his voice.

Music plays. ENOBARBUS *places each man in position, hand in hand.*

BOY

(singing) Come, you king of the vine, plump Bacchus, with your pink eyes. Our troubles are drowned in your vats. We'll crown ourselves with wreathes of grapes.

ALL

(singing) Give us cups until the world spins! Give us cups until the world spins!

CAESAR

How can you top that? Good night, Pompey. *(to* ANTONY*)* Dear brother-in-law, let's leave together. This frivolity isn't appropriate to the serious purpose that brought us here. Noble lords, let's say good night. We've all gotten red in the face. Even the strong Enobarbus isn't immune to the effects of wine, and I'm tongue-tied myself. This wild party has almost turned us all into clowns. What more need I say? Good night. Good Antony, shake my hand.

POMPEY

We'll have a rematch at your feast on shore.

ANTONY
125   And shall, sir. Give 's your hand.

POMPEY
              O Antony, You have my father's house.
              But what? We are friends. Come, down into the boat.

ENOBARBUS
              Take heed you fall not.

                          Exeunt all but MENAS *and* ENOBARBUS

                          Menas, I'll not on shore.

MENAS
              No, to my cabin. These drums, these trumpets, flutes!
                  What!
130   Let Neptune hear we bid a loud farewell
              To these great fellows. Sound and be hanged, sound out!

              Sound a flourish, with drums

ENOBARBUS
              Hoo! says 'a. There's my cap.

              He flings it in the air

MENAS
              Hoo! Noble captain, come.

                                  Exeunt

ANTONY

Yes, we will. Let's shake on it.

POMPEY

Oh, Antony, even if you've taken my father's house, what is that to me? We're friends! Come, this way to the rowboat.

ENOBARBUS

Be careful not to fall in.

Everyone exits except MENAS *and* ENOBARBUS.

Menas, I'm not going back on shore.

MENAS

No, come to my cabin. We'll have the musicians play drums, trumpets, flutes. What do you say? We'll make Neptune hear us bid a loud good night to these great men. Play and be damned. Play loud!

Neptune = Roman god of the sea

Trumpets and drums play a fanfare.

ENOBARBUS

Hooray, I say. There's my hat!

He throws his hat in the air.

MENAS

Hooray! Come on, noble captain.

They exit.

ACT THREE

SCENE 1

Enter VENTIDIUS *as it were in triumph, the dead body of Pacorus borne before him, with* SILIUS, *and other Romans, officers, and soldiers*

VENTIDIUS
Now, darting Parthia, art thou struck, and now
Pleased fortune does of Marcus Crassus' death
Make me revenger. Bear the King's son's body
Before our army. Thy Pacorus, Orodes,
⁵ Pays this for Marcus Crassus.

SILIUS
                     Noble Ventidius,
Whilst yet with Parthian blood thy sword is warm,
The fugitive Parthians follow. Spur through Media,
Mesopotamia, and the shelters whither
The routed fly. So thy grand captain, Antony,
¹⁰ Shall set thee on triumphant chariots and
Put garlands on thy head.

VENTIDIUS
                  O Silius, Silius,
I have done enough. A lower place, note well,
May make too great an act. For learn this, Silius:
Better to leave undone than by our deed
¹⁵ Acquire too high a fame when him we serve's away.
Caesar and Antony have ever won
More in their officer than person. Sossius,
One of my place in Syria, his lieutenant,
For quick accumulation of renown,
²⁰ Which he achieved by th' minute, lost his favor.
Who does i' th' wars more than his captain can
Becomes his captain's captain; and ambition,
The soldier's virtue, rather makes choice of loss

ACT THREE

SCENE 1

The dead body of Pacorus is carried in, followed by the triumphant entrance of VENTIDIUS, *with* SILIUS *and soldiers.*

VENTIDIUS

Now I've paid you back, Parthia, and gotten revenge for Marcus Crassus' death. Carry King Orodes' son at the front of our army, so all the Parthians will know— Orodes, Pacorus pays for Marcus Crassus!

SILIUS

Noble Ventidius, while your sword is still warm with the blood of slain Parthians, why not finish the job? The Parthians retreat. Go after them. Chase them down if you have to track them through Media, Mesopotamia, or any other places they may go to hide. Then our great general, Antony, will commend you.

VENTIDIUS

Oh, Silius, Silius, I've done enough. A subordinate may exceed his authority. You must understand, Silius, that it's better to leave something undone than achieve too much fame in your superior's absence. Caesar and Antony have always achieved more by delegating authority to their officers than by leading their troops in person. Sossius, an officer that held the same position in Syria as I do here, achieved great distinction very quickly but lost Antony's support as a result. A man who achieves more in war than his captain does becomes his captain's rival. Ambition is a good quality in a soldier, but it proves detrimental rather than beneficial when used to surpass his superiors. I could

Than gain which darkens him.
25   I could do more to do Antonius good,
But 'twould offend him, and in his offense
Should my performance perish.

SILIUS

Thou hast, Ventidius, that
Without the which a soldier and his sword
30   Grants scarce distinction. Thou wilt write to Antony?

VENTIDIUS

I'll humbly signify what in his name,
That magical word of war, we have effected:
How with his banners and his well-paid ranks
The ne'er-yet-beaten horse of Parthia
35   We have jaded out o' th' field.

SILIUS

                 Where is he now?

VENTIDIUS

He purposeth to Athens, whither, with what haste
The weight we must convey with's will permit,
We shall appear before him. *(to the soliders)* On, there. Pass
    along!

                          Exeunt

do more to help Antony, but to do so would insult him. And by insulting him, I would lose credit for the good I have done him already.

SILIUS

A soldier is just a tool, like his sword, unless he has your qualities, Ventidius. Are you going to write Antony about this?

VENTIDIUS

I'll modestly tell him what I have done in his name— that's the magical wording these days. I'll write how, under his flag and with his well-paid troops, we have beaten the formerly unvanquished Parthia.

SILIUS

Where's Antony now?

VENTIDIUS

He plans to go to Athens. We must arrive there before him, as quickly as our baggage train will allow us. *(to the soldiers)* Get a move on!

They all exit.

ACT 3, SCENE 2

Enter AGRIPPA *at one door,* ENOBARBUS *at another*

AGRIPPA
What, are the brothers parted?

ENOBARBUS
They have dispatched with Pompey; he is gone.
The other three are sealing. Octavia weeps
To part from Rome. Caesar is sad, and Lepidus,
Since Pompey's feast, as Menas says, is troubled
With the greensickness.

AGRIPPA
                                'Tis a noble Lepidus.

ENOBARBUS
A very fine one. Oh, how he loves Caesar!

AGRIPPA
Nay, but how dearly he adores Mark Antony!

ENOBARBUS
Caesar? Why, he's the Jupiter of men.

AGRIPPA
What's Antony? The god of Jupiter.

ENOBARBUS
Spake you of Caesar? How, the nonpareil!

AGRIPPA
O Antony, O thou Arabian bird!

ENOBARBUS
Would you praise Caesar, say "Caesar." Go no further.

ACT 3, SCENE 2

AGRIPPA enters through one door and ENOBARBUS enters through another.

AGRIPPA

Did the brothers-in-law leave?

ENOBARBUS

They finished their business with Pompey, and Pompey has left. Now the three triumvirs are putting their official seals on the treaty. Octavia weeps at the thought of leaving Rome. Caesar is in a sober mood. And Menas reports that Lepidus has been hungover since Pompey's party.

AGRIPPA

A pun: lepidus means "elegant" in Latin.

That Lepidus is an elegant man.

ENOBARBUS

He's a stylish man. And how he loves Caesar!

AGRIPPA

Yes, but how he adores Mark Antony!

ENOBARBUS

Enobarbus and Agrippa mock Lepidus' excessive flattery.

Caesar? He's a god of a man.

AGRIPPA

Then what's Antony? A god of a god?

ENOBARBUS

Are you talking about Caesar? He's without equal!

AGRIPPA

phoenix = mythical bird, symbol of immortality

Oh, Antony! Oh, you phoenix!

ENOBARBUS

If you want to praise Caesar, just say his name—that's all the praise that's necessary.

AGRIPPA
　　　Indeed, he plied them both with excellent praises.

ENOBARBUS
15　　　But he loves Caesar best; yet he loves Antony.
　　　Hoo! Hearts, tongues, figures, scribes, bards, poets, cannot
　　　Think, speak, cast, write, sing, number—hoo!—
　　　His love to Antony. But as for Caesar,
　　　Kneel down, kneel down, and wonder.

AGRIPPA
　　　　　　　　　　　　　　　　　　　　Both he loves.

ENOBARBUS
20　　　They are his shards, and he their beetle.

　　　Trumpets within

　　　　　　　　　　　　　　　　　　　　　　So,
　　　This is to horse. Adieu, noble Agrippa.

AGRIPPA
　　　Good fortune, worthy soldier, and farewell.

　　　Enter CAESAR, ANTONY, LEPIDUS, *and* OCTAVIA

ANTONY
　　　No further, sir.

CAESAR
　　　You take from me a great part of myself;
25　　　Use me well in 't.—Sister, prove such a wife
　　　As my thoughts make thee, and as my farthest bond
　　　Shall pass on thy approof.—Most noble Antony,
　　　Let not the piece of virtue, which is set
　　　Betwixt us as the cement of our love,
30　　　To keep it builded, be the ram to batter
　　　The fortress of it. For better might we

AGRIPPA

He certainly flattered them both with extravagant compliments.

ENOBARBUS

He loves Caesar best, but he also loves Antony. Oh! No one can describe or fathom Lepidus' love for Antony! Hearts cannot think it, tongues cannot speak it, measurements cannot calculate it, scribes cannot write it, bards cannot sing it, and poets cannot make verses about it. But when it comes to Caesar, Lepidus' love approaches the awestruck wonder of a worshipper.

AGRIPPA

He loves them both.

ENOBARBUS

Shard-beetles make their home in dung heaps.

They are his dung, and he their beetle.

Trumpets sound.

So, there's the signal to ride. Good-bye, noble Agrippa.

AGRIPPA

Good luck, worthy soldier, and good-bye.

CAESAR, ANTONY, LEPIDUS, *and* OCTAVIA *enter.*

ANTONY

You can't go any further with us, sir.

CAESAR

You take an important part of myself with you. Treat it well . . . . Sister, be the kind of wife I hope you will be, and that this great contract rests upon your being . . . Gracious Antony, don't let my sister, this epitome of virtue that connects us, become the reason we separate.

Have loved without this mean, if on both parts
This be not cherished.

ANTONY
                                        Make me not offended
In your distrust.

CAESAR
                              I have said.

ANTONY
                                              You shall not find,
35   Though you be therein curious, the least cause
For what you seem to fear. So the gods keep you
And make the hearts of Romans serve your ends.
We will here part.

CAESAR
Farewell, my dearest sister, fare thee well.
40   The elements be kind to thee and make
Thy spirits all of comfort! Fare thee well.

OCTAVIA
My noble brother!

She weeps

ANTONY
The April's in her eyes; it is love's spring,
And these the showers to bring it on. *(to* **OCTAVIA***)* Be
          cheerful.

OCTAVIA
45   *(to* **CAESAR***)* Sir, look well to my husband's house, and—

CAESAR
What, Octavia?

OCTAVIA
                          I'll tell you in your ear.

She and **CAESAR** *walk aside*

If you and I don't value her equally, it would be better for us to work out our differences without her.

ANTONY

Don't insult me with your distrust.

CAESAR

I mean what I say.

ANTONY

You won't find any cause for anxiety, even if you look for one. So, may the gods protect you and change the hearts of the Romans so that they turn and give you their support. We'll leave you here.

CAESAR

Good-bye, my dearest sister, good-bye. I hope you have good weather to set your mind at ease. Farewell.

OCTAVIA

My noble brother!

She begins to cry.

ANTONY

Her eyes are like April: full of showers. But they'll flower into love. *(to* OCTAVIA*)* Be cheerful.

OCTAVIA

(to CAESAR*)* Take care of my former husband's property, and—

CAESAR

What is it, Octavia?

OCTAVIA

I'll tell you privately.

She and CAESAR *move apart from the group, and she whispers to him.*

ANTONY
Her tongue will not obey her heart, nor can
Her heart inform her tongue—the swan's-down feather
That stands upon the swell at the full of tide
50   And neither way inclines.

ENOBARBUS
(aside to AGRIPPA*)* Will Caesar weep?

AGRIPPA
(aside to ENOBARBUS*)* He has a cloud in 's face.

ENOBARBUS
(aside to AGRIPPA*)* He were the worse for that, were he a
            horse;
So is he, being a man.

AGRIPPA
    (aside to ENOBARBUS*)* Why, Enobarbus,
55   When Antony found Julius Caesar dead,
He cried almost to roaring, and he wept
When at Philippi he found Brutus slain.

ENOBARBUS
(aside to AGRIPPA*)* That year indeed he was troubled with a
            rheum.
What willingly he did confound he wailed,
60   Believe 't, till I wept too.

CAESAR
        (coming forward with OCTAVIA*)* No, sweet Octavia,
You shall hear from me still. The time shall not
Outgo my thinking on you.

ANTONY
                        Come, sir, come,
I'll wrestle with you in my strength of love.
Look, here I have you.

Embraces him

                    Thus I let you go
65   And give you to the gods.

ANTONY

> She won't say what she's feeling, and she can't understand her feelings. She's balanced uneasily, like a feather on the swell of a great wave—she won't move, even though her situation is about to change.

ENOBARBUS

> (*aside to* AGRIPPA) Do you think Caesar will cry?

AGRIPPA

> (*aside to* ENOBARBUS) He does look like it.

ENOBARBUS

> (*aside to* AGRIPPA) If he were a horse, watery eyes would lower his value. Men aren't supposed to cry, either.

AGRIPPA

> (*aside to* ENOBARBUS) Why, Enobarbus, when Antony saw that Julius Caesar was dead, he cried terribly. And he wept when he found that Brutus had been killed at Philippi.

ENOBARBUS

> (*aside to* AGRIPPA) He certainly did have rheumy eyes that year. Whenever he had to kill, he cried—it's true!—until I cried too.

CAESAR

> (*returning with* OCTAVIA) Don't worry, sweet Octavia, I'll always write to you, and I'll think about you all the time.

ANTONY

> Come here, sir. I'll wrestle with you out of love. See, now I have you.

> *They embrace.*

> And thus I let you go and give you to the gods.

CAESAR
                    Adieu. Be happy.

LEPIDUS
(*to* ANTONY) Let all the number of the stars give light
To thy fair way.

CAESAR
                    Farewell, farewell.

Kisses OCTAVIA

ANTONY
                              Farewell.

Trumpets sound. Exeunt

NO FEAR SHAKESPEARE

CAESAR

Good-bye. Be happy.

LEPIDUS

(to ANTONY*)* May every star light your path.

CAESAR

Farewell, farewell.

He kisses OCTAVIA.

ANTONY

Farewell.

Trumpets sound a fanfare as they exit.

ACT 3, SCENE 3

Enter CLEOPATRA, CHARMIAN, IRAS, *and* ALEXAS

CLEOPATRA
Where is the fellow?

ALEXAS
                    Half afeard to come.

CLEOPATRA
Go to, go to.—Come hither, sir.

Enter the MESSENGER *as before*

ALEXAS
                              Good majesty,
Herod of Jewry dare not look upon you
But when you are well pleased.

CLEOPATRA
                         That Herod's head
5   I'll have! But how? When Antony is gone,
Through whom I might command it? *(to* MESSENGER*)*
                    Come thou near.

MESSENGER
Most gracious majesty!

CLEOPATRA
                         Didst thou behold Octavia?

MESSENGER
Ay, dread Queen.

CLEOPATRA
                    Where?

MESSENGER
                         Madam, in Rome.
I looked her in the face, and saw her led
10   Between her brother and Mark Antony.

CLEOPATRA
Is she as tall as me?

ACT 3, SCENE 3

CLEOPATRA, CHARMIAN, IRAS, *and* ALEXAS *enter.*

CLEOPATRA

Where is that messenger?

ALEXAS

He's afraid to come in.

CLEOPATRA

Oh, come on.—Come here, sir.

The MESSENGER *enters.*

ALEXAS

Gracious Queen, even Herod of Judea wouldn't dare look at you unless you were in a good mood.

CLEOPATRA

I'll have Herod's head chopped off! But now that Antony's gone, who will do it for me? *(to* MESSENGER*)* Come closer.

MESSENGER

Most formidable Queen!

CLEOPATRA

Did you see Octavia?

MESSENGER

Yes, revered Queen.

CLEOPATRA

Where?

MESSENGER

In Rome, Madam. I saw her face as she walked with her brother and Mark Antony.

CLEOPATRA

Is she as tall as I am?

MESSENGER
She is not, madam.

CLEOPATRA
Didst hear her speak? Is she shrill-tongued or low?

MESSENGER
Madam, I heard her speak. She is low-voiced.

CLEOPATRA
That's not so good. He cannot like her long.

CHARMIAN
15 Like her? O Isis, 'tis impossible.

CLEOPATRA
I think so, Charmian. Dull of tongue, and dwarfish.—
What majesty is in her gait? Remember,
If e'er thou looked'st on majesty.

MESSENGER
She creeps.
Her motion and her station are as one.
20 She shows a body rather than a life,
A statue than a breather.

CLEOPATRA
Is this certain?

MESSENGER
Or I have no observance.

CHARMIAN
Three in Egypt
Cannot make better note.

CLEOPATRA
He's very knowing,
I do perceive 't. There's nothing in her yet.
25 The fellow has good judgment.

CHARMIAN
Excellent.

CLEOPATRA
(to MESSENGER*)* Guess at her years, I prithee.

MESSENGER

She is not, madam.

CLEOPATRA

Did you hear her speak? Is her voice pitched high or low?

MESSENGER

Madam, I heard her speak. She has a low-pitched voice.

CLEOPATRA

That's not in her favor. He can't like her very long.

CHARMIAN

Like her? Oh, Isis, that's impossible.

CLEOPATRA

You're right, Charmian. She's both dull-spoken and dwarfishly little.—Did she carry herself with majesty? Compare her to any memory you might have of royalty.

MESSENGER

She creeps along. Moving or standing still, her bearing is about the same. She has a body, not a life. She's more like a statue than a living, breathing human being.

CLEOPATRA

Is this true?

MESSENGER

If not, then I have no powers of observation.

CHARMIAN

There aren't three people in all of Egypt who could do better.

CLEOPATRA

He's very observant. I can tell. She doesn't have anything going for her so far. This messenger is wise.

CHARMIAN

Very wise.

CLEOPATRA

(to MESSENGER) How old do you think she is?

MESSENGER
Madam, she was a widow—

CLEOPATRA
Widow? Charmian, hark.

MESSENGER
And I do think she's thirty.

CLEOPATRA
30 Bear'st thou her face in mind? Is 't long or round?

MESSENGER
Round, even to faultiness.

CLEOPATRA
For the most part, too, they are foolish that are so.
Her hair, what color?

MESSENGER
Brown, madam, and her forehead
35 As low as she would wish it.

CLEOPATRA
          (giving money)   There's gold for thee.
Thou must not take my former sharpness ill.
I will employ thee back again; I find thee
Most fit for business. Go make thee ready;
Our letters are prepared.

                              Exit MESSENGER

CHARMIAN
                    A proper man.

CLEOPATRA
40 Indeed, he is so. I repent me much
That so I harried him. Why, methinks, by him,
This creature's no such thing.

CHARMIAN
                              Nothing, madam.

CLEOPATRA
The man hath seen some majesty and should know.

MESSENGER

She was a widow previously, madam.

CLEOPATRA

A widow? Do you hear that, Charmian?

MESSENGER

And I think she's at least thirty.

CLEOPATRA

Do you remember her face? Was it long or round?

MESSENGER

Round enough to be unattractive.

CLEOPATRA

Usually that means a person is foolish. What color is her hair?

MESSENGER

Brown, madam, and she wouldn't want her forehead to be any lower.

CLEOPATRA

Here's gold for you. You mustn't hold my earlier outburst against me. I'll hire you again to go back to Rome. I find that you're very good at this kind of work. Go, prepare to travel. My letters are ready to go.

The **MESSENGER** *exits.*

CHARMIAN

He's an admirable man.

CLEOPATRA

He certainly is. I'm very sorry I was so hard on him. Why, from what he says, Octavia isn't worth getting upset over.

CHARMIAN

Not a bit, madam.

CLEOPATRA

This man's been around royalty. He should recognize it when he sees it.

CHARMIAN

    Hath he seen majesty? Isis else defend,
45   And serving you so long!

CLEOPATRA

    I have one thing more to ask him yet, good Charmian—
    But 'tis no matter; thou shalt bring him to me
    Where I will write. All may be well enough.

CHARMIAN

    I warrant you, madam.

                                      Exeunt

CHARMIAN

> Been around royalty! Isis forbid it were otherwise, since he's been in your service so long.

CLEOPATRA

> I want to ask him one more thing, Charmian. But it's not important. Bring him to my writing room. Everything may still be all right.

CHARMIAN

> I assure you it is, madam.

They exit.

ACT 3, SCENE 4

Enter ANTONY *and* OCTAVIA

ANTONY
Nay, nay, Octavia, not only that—
That were excusable, that and thousands more
Of semblable import—but he hath waged
New wars 'gainst Pompey; made his will, and read it
5   To public ear;
Spoke scantly of me; when perforce he could not
But pay me terms of honor, cold and sickly
He vented them, most narrow measure lent me.
When the best hint was given him, he not took 't,
10   Or did it from his teeth.

OCTAVIA
                    O my good lord,
Believe not all, or, if you must believe,
Stomach not all. A more unhappy lady,
If this division chance, ne'er stood between,
Praying for both parts.
15   The good gods will mock me presently,
When I shall pray "O bless my lord and husband!"
Undo that prayer by crying out as loud
"O bless my brother!" Husband win, win brother
Prays and destroys the prayer; no midway
20   'Twixt these extremes at all.

ANTONY
                    Gentle Octavia,
Let your best love draw to that point which seeks
Best to preserve it. If I lose mine honor,
I lose myself; better I were not yours
Than yours so branchless. But, as you requested,
25   Yourself shall go between 's. The meantime, lady,
I'll raise the preparation of a war

ACT 3, SCENE 4

ANTONY *and* OCTAVIA *enter.*

ANTONY

No, no, Octavia, it's not only that. That would be excusable—that and a thousand other offenses like it. But Caesar has gone and waged a new war against Pompey. He made his will and read it in a public assembly. He hardly refers to me at all, though official decisions are supposed to be made jointly. When he can't avoid mentioning my services to the state, he minimizes them as much as possible. When situations arise when it would be natural to emphasize my due credit, he either ignores them or only pays me lip service.

Roman politicians could gain popularity among the common people by writing a will that included bequests in their favor, such as sums of money, parkland, or orchards dedicated to their use.

OCTAVIA

Oh, dear husband, don't believe everything you hear—or if you must believe it, don't let it all make you angry. No lady could be more miserable than I if you two disagree. I'll be left in the middle, praying for both sides. The good gods will laugh at me when on the one hand I pray for my husband and on the other for my brother. "Let my husband win!" "Let my brother win!" One prayer cancels out the other. There's no middle ground between these two extremes.

ANTONY

Gentle Octavia, support the one that supports you. If I'm defeated, I lose my reputation. If I lose my reputation, I lose myself. It would be better for you to have no husband than a husband who lacks honor. However, as you requested, you may go and try to negotiate with your brother. In the meantime, I'll raise an

Shall stain your brother. Make your soonest haste;
So your desires are yours.

OCTAVIA

                              Thanks to my lord.
The Jove of power make me most weak, most weak,
30   Your reconciler! Wars 'twixt you twain would be
As if the world should cleave, and that slain men
Should solder up the rift.

ANTONY

When it appears to you where this begins,
Turn your displeasure that way, for our faults
35   Can never be so equal that your love
Can equally move with them. Provide your going;
Choose your own company and command what cost
Your heart has mind to.

                                        Exeunt

army that will surpass his. Go as soon as possible, so your prayers may be answered the sooner.

OCTAVIA

Thank you, my lord. May the god of power make me, the weakest of the weak, your mediator. A war between you two would split the very world, and the bodies of your slaughtered soldiers would have to fill the chasm between.

ANTONY

When you find out who started this disagreement, turn your anger upon them. Our faults can't be so alike that you would judge us similarly. Order supplies for your trip and choose your traveling companions. Spend as much as you like.

They exit.

ACT 3, SCENE 5

Enter ENOBARBUS *and* EROS

ENOBARBUS
How now, friend Eros!

EROS
There's strange news come, sir.

ENOBARBUS
What, man?

EROS
Caesar and Lepidus have made wars upon Pompey.

ENOBARBUS
5   This is old. What is the success?

EROS
Caesar, having made use of him in the wars 'gainst Pompey, presently denied him rivality, would not let him partake in the glory of the action, and, not resting here, accuses him of letters he had formerly wrote to Pompey; upon his own
10   appeal seizes him. So the poor third is up, till death enlarge his confine.

ENOBARBUS
·   Then, world, thou hast a pair of chaps, no more,
And throw between them all the food thou hast,
They'll grind the one the other. Where's Antony?

EROS
15   He's walking in the garden—*(imitating anger)* thus, and
            spurns
The rush that lies before him; cries, "Fool Lepidus!"
And threats the throat of that his officer
That murdered Pompey.

ACT 3, SCENE 5

ENOBARBUS *and* EROS *enter.*

ENOBARBUS

How goes it, friend Eros?

EROS

Some startling news has just arrived, sir.

ENOBARBUS

What news, man?

EROS

Caesar and Lepidus declared war against Pompey.

ENOBARBUS

That's old news. Who's winning?

EROS

Caesar used Lepidus in the war, but as soon as it was over, Lepidus was expelled from the triumvirate. He wasn't allowed any of the glory of the victory, and he was accused of treasonous correspondence with Pompey. On the basis of Caesar's accusation alone, Lepidus was imprisoned. So the weak third of the triumvirate is imprisoned until death frees him.

ENOBARBUS

So now the world will only be devoured by two sets of jaws—Caesar's and Antony's. And even if you throw everything you possess to the two of them, they'll battle each other to the death to have it all. Where's Antony?

EROS

He's walking in the garden, like this *(imitating anger).* And he kicks the leaves on the path, exclaiming, "Lepidus, you fool!" Then he threatens to kill the officer who murdered Pompey.

Pompey was killed by one of Antony's officers, Titius, during his campaign for Antony's territories. Some historians believe that Titius acted on Antony's specific order.

ENOBARBUS
                              Our great navy's rigged.

EROS
        For Italy and Caesar. More, Domitius:
20   My lord desires you presently. My news
        I might have told hereafter.

ENOBARBUS
                                    'Twill be naught,
        But let it be. Bring me to Antony.

EROS
        Come, sir.

                                                    Exeunt

ENOBARBUS

Antony's grand navy is prepared.

EROS

To sail to Italy and Caesar. Another thing, Domitius: Antony wants to see you now. I should have waited to tell you my news.

ENOBARBUS

It won't be that important. But never mind. Take me to Antony.

EROS

Come with me, sir.

They exit.

ACT 3, SCENE 6

Enter AGRIPPA, MECAENAS, *and* CAESAR

CAESAR
 Contemning Rome, he has done all this and more
 In Alexandria. Here's the manner of 't:
 I' th' marketplace, on a tribunal silvered,
 Cleopatra and himself in chairs of gold
5 Were publicly enthroned. At the feet sat
 Caesarion, whom they call my father's son,
 And all the unlawful issue that their lust
 Since then hath made between them. Unto her
 He gave the stablishment of Egypt, made her
10 Of lower Syria, Cyprus, Lydia,
 Absolute Queen.

MAECENAS
       This in the public eye?

CAESAR
 I' th' common showplace, where they exercise.
 His sons he there proclaimed the kings of kings:
 Great Media, Parthia, and Armenia
15 He gave to Alexander; to Ptolemy he assigned
 Syria, Cilicia, and Phoenicia. She
 In th' habiliments of the goddess Isis
 That day appeared, and oft before gave audience,
 As 'tis reported, so.

MAECENAS
20 Let Rome be thus informed.

AGRIPPA
 Who, queasy with his insolence already,
 Will their good thoughts call from him.

CAESAR
 The people knows it, and have now received
 His accusations.

ACT 3, SCENE 6

AGRIPPA, MAECENAS, *and* CAESAR *enter.*

CAESAR

In Alexandria he condemned Rome, and that's not all. This is what happened: he and Cleopatra sat on chairs of gold on a silver-covered stage in the marketplace. Caesarion—whom they call my father's son—and all their illegitimate children sat at their feet. Antony confirmed her possession of Egypt and made her absolute Queen of lower Syria, Cyprus, and Lydia.

Julius Caesar was Octavius Caesar's adopted father (biologically, he was his uncle).

MAECENAS

He did this in public?

CAESAR

In the public arena, where they perform sporting events. He proclaimed his sons to be kings of kings. He gave Media, Parthia, and Armenia to Alexander. He gave Syria, Cilicia, and Phoenicia to Ptolemy. Cleopatra was dressed like the goddess Isis. They say she often attended her public functions like that.

MAECENAS

Let's send this news to Rome.

AGRIPPA

The Roman people are fed up with his arrogance already. They'll abandon him completely when they hear this.

CAESAR

The people have heard it already, and they've been told of his accusations.

AGRIPPA

                    Who does he accuse?

CAESAR

25   Caesar, and that, having in Sicily
        Sextus Pompeius spoiled, we had not rated him
        His part o' th' isle. Then does he say he lent me
        Some shipping, unrestored. Lastly, he frets
        That Lepidus of the triumvirate
30   Should be deposed, and, being, that we detain
        All his revenue.

AGRIPPA

                    Sir, this should be answered.

CAESAR

        'Tis done already, and the messenger gone.
        I have told him, Lepidus was grown too cruel,
        That he his high authority abused
35   And did deserve his change. For what I have conquered,
        I grant him part; but then, in his Armenia,
        And other of his conquered kingdoms, I
        Demand the like.

MAECENAS

                    He'll never yield to that.

CAESAR

        Nor must not then be yielded to in this.

        Enter OCTAVIA *with her train*

OCTAVIA

40   Hail, Caesar, and my lord! Hail, most dear Caesar!

CAESAR

        That ever I should call thee castaway!

OCTAVIA

        You have not called me so, nor have you cause.

AGRIPPA

Who does he accuse?

CAESAR

He accuses me of withholding his share of Sextus Pompeius' possessions, which we seized in Sicily. Then he says I didn't return some ships he loaned me. Finally, he criticizes the deposing of Lepidus, and then goes on to accuse me of keeping all of Lepidus' property for myself.

AGRIPPA

Sir, these accusations should be answered.

CAESAR

It has been done already, and the messenger is on his way. I answered that Lepidus had become too brutal and abused his position. For this he deserved to be deposed. As for what I seized in the wars, I granted that Antony should have a share. But I also demanded my share of his acquisitions in Armenia and the other conquered kingdoms.

MAECENAS

He'll never agree to that.

CAESAR

Then we won't agree to his demands.

OCTAVIA *enters with her attendants.*

OCTAVIA

Greetings, Caesar, my lord! Greetings, dearest Caesar!

CAESAR

Oh, to think you've been rejected!

OCTAVIA

You've never thought of me like that, and you have no reason to.

CAESAR
Why have you stol'n upon us thus? You come not
Like Caesar's sister. The wife of Antony
45 Should have an army for an usher and
The neighs of horse to tell of her approach
Long ere she did appear. The trees by th' way
Should have borne men, and expectation fainted,
Longing for what it had not. Nay, the dust
50 Should have ascended to the roof of heaven,
Raised by your populous troops. But you are come
A market-maid to Rome and have prevented
The ostentation of our love, which, left unshown,
Is often left unloved. We should have met you
55 By sea and land, supplying every stage
With an augmented greeting.

OCTAVIA
                                        Good my lord,
To come thus was I not constrained, but did it
On my free will. My lord, Mark Antony,
Hearing that you prepared for war, acquainted
60 My grievèd ear withal, whereon I begged
His pardon for return.

CAESAR
                                  Which soon he granted,
Being an obstruct 'tween his lust and him.

OCTAVIA
Do not say so, my lord.

CAESAR
                                  I have eyes upon him,
And his affairs come to me on the wind.
65 Where is he now?

OCTAVIA
My lord, in Athens.

CAESAR
No, my most wrongèd sister. Cleopatra
Hath nodded him to her. He hath given his empire

CAESAR

> Then why did you travel so quietly? You didn't arrive like Caesar's sister. Antony's wife should have an army to escort her, with neighing horses to announce her arrival long before she appears. The trees along the road should have been filled with eager spectators. Crowds should have been faint with excitement waiting to see you. The dust from your attending troops should have risen to heaven. But you've arrived like a common maid bringing goods to a Roman market. You've kept me from displaying my love—and when love is not shown, it's often not felt. I would have met you by sea and again by land. At each stage of your trip there would have been a more spectacular greeting.

OCTAVIA

> My good lord, I wasn't forced to travel like this. It was my choice. Mark Antony heard that you were preparing to wage war on him. When he gave me this news, I begged him to let me visit you.

CAESAR

> Which he quickly allowed, given that you're an obstacle to his lust.

OCTAVIA

> Don't say that, my lord.

CAESAR

> I've kept track of him, and reports of his affairs arrive on every ship. Where do you think he is now?

OCTAVIA

> He's in Athens, my lord.

CAESAR

> No, he's not. You've been deceived. Cleopatra summoned him. He's given his empire to a whore, and

Up to a whore; who now are levying
70   The kings o' th' earth for war. He hath assembled
Bocchus, the King of Libya; Archelaus,
Of Cappadocia; Philadelphos, King
Of Paphlagonia; the Thracian king, Adallas;
King Manchus of Arabia; King of Pont;
75   Herod of Jewry; Mithridates, King
Of Comagen; Polemon and Amyntas,
The Kings of Mede and Lycaonia,
With a more larger list of scepters.

OCTAVIA
Ay me, most wretched,
80   That have my heart parted betwixt two friends
That does afflict each other!

CAESAR
                              Welcome hither.
Your letters did withhold our breaking forth
Till we perceived both how you were wrong led
And we in negligent danger. Cheer your heart.
85   Be you not troubled with the time, which drives
O'er your content these strong necessities,
But let determined things to destiny
Hold unbewailed their way. Welcome to Rome,
Nothing more dear to me. You are abused
90   Beyond the mark of thought, and the high gods,
To do you justice, makes his ministers
Of us and those that love you. Best of comfort,
And ever welcome to us.

AGRIPPA
                              Welcome, lady.

MAECENAS
Welcome, dear madam.
95   Each heart in Rome does love and pity you.

now they're gathering kings to wage a war. He's recruited Bocchus, the King of Libya; Archelaus of Cappadocia; Philadelphos, King of Paphlagonia; the Thracian king, Adallas; King Manchus of Arabia; the King of Pont; Herod, of Judea; Mithridates, King of Comagen; Polemon and Amyntas, the kings of Mede and Lycaonia, and many more.

OCTAVIA

Oh, I'm heartbroken. I'm divided between two friends who are determined to kill each other.

CAESAR

You're welcome here. I didn't write about breaking the alliance with Antony until I saw you were being misled and realized how dangerous it would be to keep postponing preparations. Cheer yourself. Don't be troubled by the present situation, the obligations of which must ruin your happiness. Don't worry about things that have already been decided by fate. Welcome home to Rome. Nothing is more precious to me than you. You have been unbelievably abused, and now the gods make us the dispensers of justice. Be comforted. You will always be welcome to me.

AGRIPPA

Welcome, lady.

MAECENAS

Welcome, dear madam. Every heart in Rome loves and pities you.

Only th' adulterous Antony, most large
In his abominations, turns you off
And gives his potent regiment to a trull
That noises it against us.

OCTAVIA
                    (to CAESAR*)*   Is it so, sir?

CAESAR
100   Most certain. Sister, welcome. Pray you
Be ever known to patience. My dear'st sister!

                                        Exeunt

Only the adulterous and abominable Antony abandons you, giving his power to a whore who turns that power against us.

OCTAVIA

(to CAESAR*)* Is that true, sir?

CAESAR

It's undeniable. You are welcome here, sister. I beg you to continue to be patient. My dearest sister!

They exit.

ACT 3, SCENE 7

Enter CLEOPATRA *and* ENOBARBUS

CLEOPATRA
I will be even with thee, doubt it not.

ENOBARBUS
But why, why, why?

CLEOPATRA
Thou hast forspoke my being in these wars
And sayst it is not fit.

ENOBARBUS
                                    Well, is it, is it?

CLEOPATRA
5   Is 't not denounced against us? Why should not we
Be there in person?

ENOBARBUS
                            Well, I could reply,
If we should serve with horse and mares together,
The horse were merely lost. The mares would bear
A soldier and his horse.

CLEOPATRA
                            What is 't you say?

ENOBARBUS
10   Your presence needs must puzzle Antony,
Take from his heart, take from his brain, from 's time
What should not then be spared. He is already
Traduced for levity, and 'tis said in Rome
That Photinus, an eunuch, and your maids
15   Manage this war.

CLEOPATRA
                            Sink Rome! And their tongues rot
That speak against us! A charge we bear i' th' war,
And as the president of my kingdom will
Appear there for a man. Speak not against it.
I will not stay behind.

ACT 3, SCENE 7

CLEOPATRA *and* ENOBARBUS *enter.*

CLEOPATRA
> I'll be straight with you. Do not doubt it.

ENOBARBUS
> But why, why, why?

CLEOPATRA
> You opposed my taking part in the war. You said it wasn't proper.

ENOBARBUS
> Well, is it? Is it?

CLEOPATRA
> Isn't this war against me? Why shouldn't I be there in person?

ENOBARBUS
> Well, I could answer that if we went to war on male and female horses alike—the male horses would be totally distracted and useless. The mares would be ridden by their riders and the male horses.

CLEOPATRA
> What do you mean?

ENOBARBUS
> Antony will necessarily be distracted by your presence. You will affect his heart and his head. You'll take up time he can't afford to lose. He's already criticized for frivolous behavior. In Rome they say that your eunuch Photinus and your maids run the war.

CLEOPATRA
> Let Rome fall! May the tongues of our critics rot! I have responsibilities in this war, and as the absolute ruler of my kingdom I will carry out my duties as if I were a man. Don't argue against it. I won't stay behind.

Enter ANTONY *and* CANIDIUS

ENOBARBUS

                              Nay, I have done.
20   Here comes the Emperor.

ANTONY

                        Is it not strange, Canidius,
That from Tarentum and Brundusium
He could so quickly cut the Ionian sea
And take in Toryne?—You have heard on 't, sweet?

CLEOPATRA

      Celerity is never more admired
25   Than by the negligent.

ANTONY

                    A good rebuke,
Which might have well becomed the best of men,
To taunt at slackness.—Canidius, we will fight
With him by sea.

CLEOPATRA

               By sea, what else?

CANIDIUS

                            Why will
My lord do so?

ANTONY

            For that he dares us to 't.

ENOBARBUS
30   So hath my lord dared him to single fight.

CANIDIUS

      Ay, and to wage this battle at Pharsalia,
Where Caesar fought with Pompey. But these offers,
Which serve not for his vantage, he shakes off,
And so should you.

ENOBARBUS

                   Your ships are not well manned,
35   Your mariners are muleteers, reapers, people
Engrossed by swift impress. In Caesar's fleet

ANTONY *and* CANIDIUS *enter.*

ENOBARBUS

No, I've had my say. Here comes the Emperor.

ANTONY

Isn't it strange, Canidius, that he could cross the Ionian Sea so quickly from Tarentum and Brundusium and take Toryne?—Have you heard about this, sweet?

CLEOPATRA

No one admires speed more than the lazy.

ANTONY

That's a good reprimand, suitable for reminding even the best of men to guard against negligence. Canidius, we'll fight him at sea.

CLEOPATRA

Of course we'll fight him by sea. What else?

CANIDIUS

Why do you want to do that, my lord?

ANTONY

Because he's daring us to do it.

ENOBARBUS

So you've dared him to single combat.

CANIDIUS

Yes, and you dared Caesar to fight the battle at Pharsalia, where he fought against Pompey. But Caesar ignores offers that don't give him an advantage, and so should you.

ENOBARBUS

Your ships are not well crewed. Your sailors are mule drivers, harvesters—men who were drafted quickly and have little training. Caesar's fleet is manned by

Are those that often have 'gainst Pompey fought.
Their ships are yare, yours, heavy. No disgrace
Shall fall you for refusing him at sea,
40   Being prepared for land.

ANTONY

By sea, by sea.

ENOBARBUS
Most worthy sir, you therein throw away
The absolute soldiership you have by land,
Distract your army, which doth most consist
Of war-marked footmen, leave unexecuted
45   Your own renownèd knowledge, quite forego
The way which promises assurance, and
Give up yourself merely to chance and hazard
From firm security.

ANTONY

I'll fight at sea.

CLEOPATRA
I have sixty sails, Caesar none better.

ANTONY
50   Our overplus of shipping will we burn,
And with the rest full-manned, from th' head of Actium
Beat th' approaching Caesar. But if we fail,
We then can do 't at land.

Enter a MESSENGER

Thy business?

MESSENGER
The news is true, my lord. He is descried.
55   Caesar has taken Toryne.

Exit

ANTONY
Can he be there in person? 'Tis impossible,
Strange that his power should be. Canidius,

mariners who already have experience battling Pompey. His ships are maneuverable. Yours are slow and awkward. Refusing to fight him at sea won't disgrace you. You've prepared for a land war.

ANTONY

I will fight by sea. By sea.

ENOBARBUS

Most worthy sir, if you do that you throw away all the advantages you have on land. You will have to divide your army, which mostly consists of battle-hardened foot soldiers. You will be unable to use your legendary battle knowledge. You'll be abandoning proven methods that promise victory, and instead you'll put yourself at the mercy of haphazard chance.

ANTONY

I'll fight at sea.

CLEOPATRA

I have sixty ships. Caesar doesn't have any that are better.

ANTONY

We'll burn our surplus ships and fully man the rest. We'll sail from Actium and beat Caesar as he approaches. Even if we fail at that, we can still fight him on land.

A MESSENGER *enters.*

What's your business?

MESSENGER

The news is true, my lord. Caesar has been seen. He has captured Toryne.

He exits.

ANTONY

Can Caesar be there in person? No, that's impossible. It's strange enough that his army should be there.

Our nineteen legions thou shalt hold by land,
And our twelve thousand horse. We'll to our ship.
Away, my Thetis!

Enter a SOLDIER

How now, worthy soldier?

SOLDIER
O noble Emperor, do not fight by sea!
Trust not to rotten planks. Do you misdoubt
This sword and these my wounds? Let th' Egyptians
And the Phoenicians go a-ducking. We
Have used to conquer standing on the earth
And fighting foot to foot.

ANTONY
Well, well, away.

Exeunt ANTONY, CLEOPATRA, *and* ENOBARBUS

SOLDIER
By Hercules, I think I am i' th' right.

CANIDIUS
Soldier, thou art; but his whole action grows
Not in the power on 't. So our leader's led,
And we are women's men.

SOLDIER
You keep by land
The legions and the horse whole, do you not?

CANIDIUS
Marcus Octavius, Marcus Justeius,
Publicola, and Caelius, are for sea;
But we keep whole by land. This speed of Caesar's
Carries beyond belief.

SOLDIER
While he was yet in Rome
His power went out in such distractions as
Beguiled all spies.

legion = military
division
consisting of
4,500 armored
infantrymen

Canidius, take our nineteen legions and twelve thousand horse soldiers. You must hold them on land. We'll go to our ship. Come away, Cleopatra.

A SOLDIER *enters.*

What's the news, brave soldier?

SOLDIER

Oh, don't fight by sea, noble Emperor! Don't trust rotten planks. Don't you trust my sword and these wounds? Let the Egyptians and Phoenicians go swimming. We are used to winning by standing on the earth and fighting toe to toe.

ANTONY

Well, well, let's go.

ANTONY, CLEOPATRA, *and* ENOBARBUS *exit.*

SOLDIER

By Hercules, I think I'm right.

CANIDIUS

Soldier, you are. But Antony's decisions aren't coming from his extensive experience. Our leader is being led. We are following a woman.

SOLDIER

On land you keep the legions and cavalry together, don't you?

CANIDIUS

Marcus Octavius, Marcus Justeius, Publicola, and Caelius will go by sea, but we'll keep the bulk on land. Caesar's speed defies belief.

SOLDIER

While he was still in Rome, he deployed his forces in so many different disguises that all our spies were fooled.

CANIDIUS
                         Who's his lieutenant, hear you?

SOLDIER
They say, one Taurus.

CANIDIUS
                         Well I know the man.

Enter a **MESSENGER**

MESSENGER
80   The Emperor calls Canidius.

CANIDIUS
With news the time's with labor, and throws forth
Each minute some.

                                        Exeunt

CANIDIUS

> Who's his lieutenant, do you know?

SOLDIER

> A man named Taurus, they say.

CANIDIUS

> I know the man well.

A MESSENGER *enters.*

MESSENGER

> The Emperor is calling for Canidius.

CANIDIUS

> The present time is like a woman in labor, each minute giving birth to some piece of news.

> *They exit.*

ACT 3, SCENE 8

Enter CAESAR *with his army, and* TAURUS, *marching*

CAESAR
Taurus!

TAURUS
My lord?

CAESAR
Strike not by land; keep whole. Provoke not battle
Till we have done at sea. Do not exceed
5   The prescript of this scroll.

He gives a scroll

                              Our fortune lies
Upon this jump.

                                        Exit with army

ACT 3, SCENE 8

CAESAR *enters with* TAURUS *and his army.*

CAESAR

Taurus!

TAURUS

My lord?

CAESAR

Don't attack by land. Keep the army together. Don't provoke them to battle until we have finished at sea. Don't exceed your orders as written here.

He hands TAURUS *a scroll.*

Our fate depends on this chance.

They exit.

ACT 3, SCENE 9

Enter ANTONY *and* ENOBARBUS

ANTONY
Set we our squadrons on yond side o' th' hill,
In eye of Caesar's battle, from which place
We may the number of the ships behold
And so proceed accordingly.

Exit

ACT 3, SCENE 9

ANTONY *and* ENOBARBUS *enter.*

ANTONY

Assemble our squadrons on the other side of the hill,
in sight of Caesar's navy. From there we'll be able to
see how many ships he has and plan accordingly.

They exit.

ACT 3, SCENE 10

*CANIDIUS marcheth with his land army one way over the stage,
and TAURUS, the lieutenant of CAESAR, the other way. After
their going in is heard the noise of a sea fight*

Alarum. Enter ENOBARBUS

ENOBARBUS
Naught, naught, all naught! I can behold no longer.
Th' *Antoniad*, the Egyptian admiral,
With all their sixty, fly and turn the rudder.
To see 't mine eyes are blasted.

Enter SCARUS

SCARUS
        Gods and goddesses,
5 All the whole synod of them!

ENOBARBUS
        What's thy passion?

SCARUS
The greater cantle of the world is lost
With very ignorance. We have kissed away
Kingdoms and provinces.

ENOBARBUS
       How appears the fight?

SCARUS
On our side like the tokened pestilence,
10 Where death is sure. Yon ribaudred nag of Egypt—
Whom leprosy o'ertake!—i' th' midst o' th' fight,
When vantage like a pair of twins appeared
Both as the same, or rather ours the elder,
The breeze upon her, like a cow in June,
15 Hoists sails and flies.

ACT 3, SCENE 10

CANIDIUS and his army marches one way across the stage while CAESAR's lieutenant, TAURUS, marches across the other way. After the two armies march off stage, the noise of a battle at sea is heard.

Trumpets sound a retreat. ENOBARBUS enters.

ENOBARBUS

We're ruined, ruined, ruined! I can't watch any more. The Egyptian flagship, the *Antoniad,* followed by all sixty Egyptian ships, has turned and fled. It destroyed my eyes to look upon it.

SCARUS enters.

SCARUS

Gods and goddesses—the whole congregation of them!

ENOBARBUS

What's wrong with you?

SCARUS

We have lost a major portion of the world through utter foolishness. We have kissed away entire kingdoms and provinces.

ENOBARBUS

How goes the battle?

SCARUS

Our side shows all the signs of certain defeat, which appear like the symptomatic sores of the plague. Right in the middle of the fight, just when the battle could have gone either way—actually we had a slight advantage—that immoral Egyptian nag—May she die of leprosy!—suddenly became frightened, and turned her ships around and fled.

ENOBARBUS
      That I beheld.
      Mine eyes did sicken at the sight and could not
      Endure a further view.

SCARUS
                              She once being loofed,
      The noble ruin of her magic, Antony,
20   Claps on his sea-wing and, like a doting mallard
      Leaving the fight in height, flies after her.
      I never saw an action of such shame.
      Experience, manhood, honor, ne'er before
      Did violate so itself.

ENOBARBUS
                              Alack, alack!

      Enter CANIDIUS

CANIDIUS
25   Our fortune on the sea is out of breath
      And sinks most lamentably. Had our general
      Been what he knew himself, it had gone well.
      Oh, he has given example for our flight
      Most grossly by his own!

ENOBARBUS
30   Ay, are you thereabouts? Why then, good night indeed.

CANIDIUS
      Toward Peloponnesus are they fled.

SCARUS
      'Tis easy to 't, and there I will attend
      What further comes.

                                          He exits

ENOBARBUS

> I saw that. The sight made me so sick I couldn't watch any more.

SCARUS

> Once she had turned around, the noble Antony, ruined by love, hoisted his own sails and followed her like a lovesick duck. He left the battle at the most crucial point. I never saw such a shameful act. He betrayed his own experience, manhood, and honor.

ENOBARBUS

> Terrible. Terrible.

> CANIDIUS *enters.*

CANIDIUS

> The battle on the sea is almost lost. If our general had been his old self, we would have won. Oh, with his sordid desertion, he sets the example for our own.

ENOBARBUS

> Are you considering desertion, as well? Then everything must really be finished.

CANIDIUS

> They fled toward Peloponnesus.

SCARUS

> It's easy to get there. I'll go there and ascertain their next move.

> > *He exits.*

CANIDIUS
                To Caesar will I render
My legions and my horse. Six kings already
Show me the way of yielding.

He exits

ENOBARBUS
               I'll yet follow
The wounded chance of Antony, though my reason
Sits in the wind against me.

He exits

CANIDIUS

I'll yield my legions and cavalry to Caesar. In this, I follow the examples of the six kings who have already surrendered.

He exits.

ENOBARBUS

I'll still follow Antony, even though the odds are against him and good sense tells me I should go the other way.

He exits.

ACT 3, SCENE 11

Enter ANTONY *with attendants*

ANTONY
Hark. The land bids me tread no more upon 't.
It is ashamed to bear me. Friends, come hither.
I am so lated in the world that I
Have lost my way forever. I have a ship
5   Laden with gold. Take that, divide it. Fly
And make your peace with Caesar.

ALL
                              Fly? Not we.

ANTONY
I have fled myself, and have instructed cowards
To run and show their shoulders. Friends, begone.
I have myself resolved upon a course
10   Which has no need of you. Begone.
My treasure's in the harbor. Take it. Oh,
I followed that I blush to look upon!
My very hairs do mutiny, for the white
Reprove the brown for rashness, and they them
15   For fear and doting. Friends, begone. You shall
Have letters from me to some friends that will
Sweep your way for you. Pray you, look not sad,
Nor make replies of loathness. Take the hint
Which my despair proclaims. Let that be left
20   Which leaves itself. To the seaside straightway!
I will possess you of that ship and treasure.
Leave me, I pray, a little. Pray you now,
Nay, do so, for indeed I have lost command.
Therefore I pray you. I'll see you by and by.
                    Exeunt attendants. ANTONY *sits down*

Enter CLEOPATRA, *led by* CHARMIAN, IRAS, *and* EROS

ACT 3, SCENE 11

ANTONY *enters with attendants.*

ANTONY

Listen. The earth tells me to stop walking upon it, as it's ashamed to carry me. Friends, come here. I'm completely lost. I have a ship full of treasure. Take that. Divide it. Escape and make peace with Caesar.

ALL

Flee? Not us.

ANTONY

I have already fled from my true self. I've told cowards to turn their backs on me and run. Friends, go. I've decided on a plan that doesn't require your assistance. Leave. My treasure's in the harbor; take it. Oh, I followed something I'm ashamed to look at now! Even my hair revolts. The white hairs blame the brown hairs for being irresponsible, and the brown ones blame the white ones for being spineless and foolish. Friends, go. I'll give you letters of introduction to some friends of mine who will help you. Please, don't be sad, and don't tell me how reluctant you are. Take your cues from my own despair. Abandon the person that has abandoned himself. Go to the harbor immediately! I'll give you the title to that ship and its treasure. Just give me a moment, please—only a moment. I've relinquished my authority, so please—I'll see you all before long.

The attendants exit. ANTONY *sits.*

CHARMIAN, IRAS, *and* EROS *enter, supporting* CLEOPATRA.

EROS
25   Nay, gentle madam, to him, comfort him.

IRAS
        Do, most dear Queen.

CHARMIAN
        Do. Why, what else?

CLEOPATRA
        Let me sit down. O Juno!

        She sits

ANTONY
        (seeing CLEOPATRA*)* No, no, no, no, no.

EROS
30   See you here, sir?

ANTONY
        Oh, fie, fie, fie!

CHARMIAN
        Madam!

IRAS
        Madam, O good Empress!

EROS
        Sir, sir—

ANTONY
35   *(aside)* Yes, my lord, yes. He at Philippi kept
        His sword e'en like a dancer, while I struck
        The lean and wrinkled Cassius, and 'twas I
        That the mad Brutus ended. He alone
        Dealt on lieutenantry, and no practice had
40   In the brave squares of war, yet now—no matter.

CLEOPATRA
        Ah, stand by.

EROS
                        The Queen, my lord, the Queen.

EROS

No, gentle madam, go. Comfort him.

IRAS

Yes, do, dearest Queen.

CHARMIAN

Of course you must comfort him! What else?

CLEOPATRA

Let me sit down. Oh, Juno!

Juno = queen of the Roman gods

She sits.

ANTONY

(seeing CLEOPATRA*)* No, no, no, no, no.

EROS

Do you see her, sir?

ANTONY

Oh, damn, damn, damn!

CHARMIAN

Madam!

IRAS

Madam, oh, good Empress!

EROS

Sir . . . sir . . .

ANTONY

(to himself) Yes, my lord, that's true. At Philippi, Caesar kept his sword in its sheath, like a dancer, while I commanded the armies that conquered Cassius and Brutus. Caesar fought only through lieutenants. He had no experience with the brave contests of war. But now . . . never mind.

CLEOPATRA

Ah, give us some privacy.

EROS

The Queen is here, my lord.

IRAS

Go to him, madam, speak to him.
He is unqualitied with very shame.

CLEOPATRA

Well then, sustain me. Oh!

She rises

EROS

45   Most noble sir, arise. The Queen approaches.
Her head's declined, and death will seize her but
Your comfort makes the rescue.

ANTONY

I have offended reputation,
A most unnoble swerving.

EROS

Sir, the Queen.

ANTONY

50   Oh, whither hast thou led me, Egypt? See
How I convey my shame out of thine eyes
By looking back what I have left behind
'Stroyed in dishonor.

CLEOPATRA

O my lord, my lord,
Forgive my fearful sails! I little thought
55   You would have followed.

ANTONY

Egypt, thou knew'st too well
My heart was to thy rudder tied by th' strings,
And thou shouldst tow me after. O'er my spirit
Thy full supremacy thou knew'st, and that
Thy beck might from the bidding of the gods
60   Command me.

CLEOPATRA

Oh, my pardon!

IRAS

Go to him, madam, speak to him. He's not himself because he feels so ashamed.

CLEOPATRA

Well, then, help me.

Her attendants help her to stand.

EROS

Most noble sir, stand up. The Queen is coming. She's weak and will die unless you comfort her.

ANTONY

I've destroyed my reputation, a most shameful error.

EROS

Sir, here's the Queen.

ANTONY

Oh, where have you led me, Egypt? See how I hide my shame from you by turning around? I look behind me to see my past, destroyed by dishonor.

CLEOPATRA

Oh, my lord, my lord, forgive my panic! I didn't think you would follow me.

ANTONY

Queen, you knew very well that my heart was tied to your ship and that you would pull me along with you. You knew that my spirit was completely under your control and that I would ignore the gods' orders in favor of yours.

CLEOPATRA

Oh, forgive me!

ANTONY

                                    Now I must
To the young man send humble treaties, dodge
And palter in the shifts of lowness, who
With half the bulk o' th' world played as I pleased,
Making and marring fortunes. You did know
65   How much you were my conqueror, and that
My sword, made weak by my affection, would
Obey it on all cause.

CLEOPATRA

                            Pardon, pardon!

ANTONY

Fall not a tear, I say. One of them rates
All that is won and lost. Give me a kiss.

They kiss

70   Even this repays me.—
We sent our schoolmaster. Is he come back?—
Love, I am full of lead.—*(calling)* Some wine,
Within there, and our viands! Fortune knows
We scorn her most when most she offers blows.

                                            Exeunt

ANTONY

Now I will have to send my humble proposal of peace to that young man. I've done as I pleased with half the world, making and losing fortunes, but now I negotiate from a position of weakness. You knew how far you had conquered my spirit. You knew that my sword, weakened by my love for you, would obey that love no matter what.

CLEOPATRA

Forgive me! Forgive me!

ANTONY

Don't shed even one tear. One of your tears is worth everything that was won and lost. Give me a kiss.

They kiss.

This repays me. I sent our children's schoolmaster to Caesar with our offer. Has he returned? Love, I am full of heaviness. *(calling)* Servants, bring some wine and food! We have the most contempt for fortune when it goes against us.

They exit.

ACT 3, SCENE 12

Enter CAESAR, AGRIPPA, THIDIAS, *and* DOLABELLA, *with others*

CAESAR
Let him appear that's come from Antony.
Know you him?

DOLABELLA
                    Caesar, 'tis his schoolmaster—
An argument that he is plucked, when hither
He sends so poor a pinion of his wing,
5   Which had superfluous kings for messengers
Not many moons gone by.

Enter AMBASSADOR *from Antony*

CAESAR
                    Approach and speak.

AMBASSADOR
Such as I am, I come from Antony.
I was of late as petty to his ends
As is the morn-dew on the myrtle leaf
10   To his grand sea.

CAESAR
                    Be 't so. Declare thine office.

AMBASSADOR
Lord of his fortunes he salutes thee, and
Requires to live in Egypt; which not granted,
He lessens his requests, and to thee sues
To let him breathe between the heavens and earth
15   A private man in Athens. This for him.
Next, Cleopatra does confess thy greatness,
Submits her to thy might, and of thee craves
The circle of the Ptolemies for her heirs,
Now hazarded to thy grace.

ACT 3, SCENE 12

CAESAR, AGRIPPA, THIDIAS, *and* DOLABELLA *enter,*
with others of the court.

CAESAR

Let the envoy from Antony come in. Do you know
him?

DOLABELLA

It's Antony's schoolmaster. By sending such an insignificant emissary, Antony shows us how low he has
sunk. Not so long ago, he had so many royal supporters that he sent along extra kings as messengers.

Antony's AMBASSADOR *enters.*

CAESAR

Come forward and speak.

AMBASSADOR

Humble as I am, I represent Antony. Until recently, I
was as unimportant to his affairs as the morning dew
is to the wide ocean.

CAESAR

So be it. Say what you're here for.

AMBASSADOR

He acknowledges that you are the master of his fate,
and he requests to be allowed to live in Egypt. If that
is not granted, he reduces his requests and asks only
that he be allowed to live as a private man in Athens.
That's all he asks for himself. Cleopatra recognizes
your greatness and accepts your authority. She only
asks that the crown of Egypt pass to her heirs, who are
now at your mercy.

CAESAR
                                        For Antony,
20   I have no ears to his request. The Queen
        Of audience nor desire shall fail, so she
        From Egypt drive her all-disgracèd friend
        Or take his life there. This if she perform,
        She shall not sue unheard. So to them both.

AMBASSADOR
25   Fortune pursue thee!

CAESAR
                            Bring him through the bands.

                            Exit **AMBASSADOR**, *attended*

        (to **THIDIAS***)* To try thy eloquence now 'tis time. Dispatch.
        From Antony win Cleopatra. Promise,
        And in our name, what she requires. Add more,
        From thine invention, offers. Women are not
30   In their best fortunes strong, but want will perjure
        The ne'er-touched vestal. Try thy cunning, Thidias.
        Make thine own edict for thy pains, which we
        Will answer as a law.

THIDIAS
                            Caesar, I go.

CAESAR
        Observe how Antony becomes his flaw,
35   And what thou think'st his very action speaks
        In every power that moves.

THIDIAS
                            Caesar, I shall.

                                        Exeunt

CAESAR

As for Antony, I'm not interested in his requests. I'll give the Queen a hearing and grant her requests if she either throws her dishonored friend out of Egypt or kills him. Then I'll listen to her. Give my answer to them both.

AMBASSADOR

May good luck follow you!

CAESAR

Take him safely through the lines.

The **AMBASSADOR** *exits.*

(to **THIDIAS***)* Now it's time to test your eloquence. On your way. Separate Cleopatra from Antony. In my name, promise to fulfill her petitions. You can make up additional offers, if necessary. Women aren't strong, even at their best. Hardship will make even a vestal abandon her vows. Use your ingenuity, Thidias. You can make your own conditions, which I will authorize as law.

vestal = virgin
priestess

THIDIAS

I go, Caesar.

CAESAR

Observe how Antony takes his defeat and how his attitude influences his actions.

THIDIAS

I will, Caesar.

They exit.

ACT 3, SCENE 13

Enter CLEOPATRA, ENOBARBUS, CHARMIAN, *and* IRAS

CLEOPATRA
What shall we do, Enobarbus?

ENOBARBUS
                                        Think and die.

CLEOPATRA
Is Antony or we in fault for this?

ENOBARBUS
Antony only, that would make his will
Lord of his reason. What though you fled
From that great face of war, whose several ranges
Frighted each other? Why should he follow?
The itch of his affection should not then
Have nicked his captainship at such a point
When half to half the world opposed, he being
The merèd question. 'Twas a shame no less
Than was his loss, to course your flying flags
And leave his navy gazing.

CLEOPATRA
                                        Prithee, peace.

Enter AMBASSADOR *with* ANTONY

ANTONY
Is that his answer?

AMBASSADOR
Ay, my lord.

ANTONY
The Queen shall then have courtesy, so she
Will yield us up?

AMBASSADOR
                                        He says so.

ACT 3, SCENE 13

CLEOPATRA, ENOBARBUS, CHARMIAN, *and* IRAS *enter.*

CLEOPATRA
> What are we going to do, Enobarbus?

ENOBARBUS
> Think about our situation, then die.

CLEOPATRA
> Who is to blame for this: Antony or I?

ENOBARBUS
> Only Antony was at fault. He put his desire in charge
> of his reason. So what if you ran from the battle, ter-
> rified, as ranks of ships threatened one another? Why
> should he have followed you? With half the world
> opposing the other half, it wasn't the time for Antony,
> the pivotal player, to let love distract him. To race
> after your departing ships, leaving his navy to watch,
> was a shame as great as the resulting loss.

CLEOPATRA
> Please, let's not talk about it.

The AMBASSADOR *and* ANTONY *enter.*

ANTONY
> Is that his answer?

AMBASSADOR
> Yes, my lord.

ANTONY
> The Queen will be treated fairly if she gives me up?

AMBASSADOR
> That's what he says.

ANTONY

                    Let her know 't.—
(to CLEOPATRA*)* To the boy Caesar send this grizzled head,
And he will fill thy wishes to the brim
With principalities.

CLEOPATRA

                    That head, my lord?

ANTONY

20   *(to the* AMBASSADOR*)* To him again. Tell him he wears the
            rose
Of youth upon him, from which the world should note
Something particular. His coin, ships, legions,
May be a coward's, whose ministers would prevail
Under the service of a child as soon
25   As i' th' command of Caesar. I dare him therefore
To lay his gay caparisons apart
And answer me declined, sword against sword,
Ourselves alone. I'll write it. Follow me.
                    Exeunt ANTONY *and* AMBASSADOR

ENOBARBUS

(aside) Yes, like enough, high-battled Caesar will
30   Unstate his happiness and be staged to th' show
Against a sworder! I see men's judgments are
A parcel of their fortunes, and things outward
Do draw the inward quality after them
To suffer all alike. That he should dream,
35   Knowing all measures, the full Caesar will
Answer his emptiness! Caesar, thou hast subdued
His judgment too.

Enter a SERVANT

SERVANT

                    A messenger from Caesar.

ANTONY

Tell her. *(to* CLEOPATRA*)* If you send my aged head to that boy, Caesar, he'll give you all the kingdoms you want.

CLEOPATRA

Your head, my lord?

ANTONY

(to the AMBASSADOR*)* Go back to him. Tell him that his cheeks still bear the pink flush of youth, and that the world expects to see something remarkable from him. His treasure, his navy, and his armies might belong to a coward, and his ministers might be able to succeed just as well on behalf of a child as under the command of Caesar. Therefore, I dare him to lay aside his fancy trappings and meet this old man in single combat, sword against sword, just the two of us. I'll write the challenge. Follow me.

ANTONY *and the* AMBASSADOR *exit.*

ENOBARBUS

(aside) Oh, that's likely! Caesar, the great commander of troops, will surely risk all he has gained in order to fight this gladiator in the public square! I see that men's judgments are tied to their fortunes, and that external factors influence a man's internal qualities, making everything suffer. How could Antony, knowing how luck stood on either side, still imagine that Caesar would respond to his nonsense! Caesar, you've conquered his judgment too.

A SERVANT *enters.*

SERVANT

A messenger has arrived from Caesar.

CLEOPATRA
What, no more ceremony? See, my women,
Against the blown rose may they stop their nose,
40   That kneeled unto the buds.—Admit him, sir.

Exit SERVANT

ENOBARBUS
(aside) Mine honesty and I begin to square.
The loyalty well held to fools does make
Our faith mere folly. Yet he that can endure
To follow with allegiance a fall'n lord
45   Does conquer him that did his master conquer
And earns a place i' th' story.

Enter THIDIAS

CLEOPATRA
                              Caesar's will?

THIDIAS
Hear it apart.

CLEOPATRA
                    None but friends. Say boldly.

THIDIAS
So haply are they friends to Antony.

ENOBARBUS
He needs as many, sir, as Caesar has,
50   Or needs not us. If Caesar please, our master
Will leap to be his friend. For us, you know
Whose he is we are, and that is Caesar's.

THIDIAS
So.—
Thus then, thou most renowned: Caesar entreats
55   Not to consider in what case thou stand'st,
Further than he is Caesar.

CLEOPATRA

With no more ceremony than that? See, ladies, how they scorn me now. They pinch their noses to avoid smelling the dying rose whose scent, as a bud, they happily inhaled. Show him in, sir.

The SERVANT *exits.*

ENOBARBUS

(aside) My integrity and I begin to contradict each other. Being loyal to a fool makes loyalty foolish. But a person who can bear to keep his allegiance to a defeated lord defeats his lord's conqueror and earns a place in history.

THIDIAS *enters.*

CLEOPATRA

What does Caesar want?

THIDIAS

It is for your ears only.

CLEOPATRA

There are only friends here. Speak confidently.

THIDIAS

So they are possibly Antony's friends.

ENOBARBUS

Sir, he should have as many as Caesar has. If he had that many friends, then he wouldn't need us. If Caesar chose, Antony would jump at the chance to be his friend. As for us, you know we are Antony's, and he is Caesar's.

THIDIAS

So be it. This, then, this is the message Caesar sends to you, famous Queen: he implores you not to be concerned about your situation. Just remember that he is Caesar.

CLEOPATRA
Go on. Right royal.

THIDIAS
He knows that you embrace not Antony
As you did love, but as you feared him.

CLEOPATRA
Oh!

THIDIAS
The scars upon your honor therefore he
60 Does pity as constrainèd blemishes,
Not as deserved.

CLEOPATRA
He is a god and knows
What is most right. Mine honor was not yielded,
But conquered merely.

ENOBARBUS
(aside) To be sure of that,
I will ask Antony. Sir, sir, thou art so leaky
65 That we must leave thee to thy sinking, for
Thy dearest quit thee.

Exit ENOBARBUS

THIDIAS
Shall I say to Caesar
What you require of him? For he partly begs
To be desired to give. It much would please him
That of his fortunes you should make a staff
70 To lean upon. But it would warm his spirits
To hear from me you had left Antony
And put yourself under his shroud,
The universal landlord.

CLEOPATRA
What's your name?

THIDIAS
My name is Thidias.

CLEOPATRA

Respectfully put. Go on.

THIDIAS

He knows that you didn't embrace Antony because you loved him, but because you feared him.

CLEOPATRA

Oh!

THIDIAS

So he regrets that any dishonorable acts were forced on you, not being performed of your own free will.

CLEOPATRA

He is like a god and knows the truth. My honor wasn't given; it was only dominated.

ENOBARBUS

(aside) I'll go get the truth of this from Antony. Sir, sir, are you so badly off that we must abandon you to your fate? Even your dearest friend has abandoned you.

ENOBARBUS *exits.*

THIDIAS

Shall I tell Caesar what you request from him? He almost begs for the opportunity to help you. It would please him very much if you would rely on his wealth and success to support you. But he would feel even better if I could tell him that you had left Antony and put yourself under his protection.

CLEOPATRA

What's your name?

THIDIAS

My name is Thidias.

CLEOPATRA
Most kind messenger,
Say to great Caesar this in deputation:
I kiss his conqu'ring hand. Tell him I am prompt
To lay my crown at 's feet, and there to kneel.
Tell him, from his all-obeying breath I hear
The doom of Egypt.

THIDIAS
'Tis your noblest course.
Wisdom and fortune combating together,
If that the former dare but what it can,
No chance may shake it. Give me grace to lay
My duty on your hand.

He kisses her hand

CLEOPATRA
Your Caesar's father oft,
When he hath mused of taking kingdoms in,
Bestowed his lips on that unworthy place
As it rained kisses.

Enter **ANTONY** *and* **ENOBARBUS**

ANTONY
Favors? By Jove that thunders!
What art thou, fellow?

THIDIAS
One that but performs
The bidding of the fullest man, and worthiest
To have command obeyed.

ENOBARBUS
You will be whipped.

CLEOPATRA

Most kind messenger, tell great Caesar that through his deputy I kiss his conquering hand. Tell him I am ready to lay my crown at his feet and kneel before him. Tell him—whose decrees are obeyed by the whole world—that I will accept the fate he chooses for Egypt.

THIDIAS

That's your most dignified course of action. When confronted with the choice between a prudent action and a risky one, a wise man should dare to do only what he can practically accomplish—if he follows this course, he will never be subjected to unpredictable chance. Allow me to pay my respects by kissing your hand.

He kisses her hand.

CLEOPATRA

When Octavius Caesar's father thought about conquering kingdoms, he rained kisses on my unworthy hand.

ANTONY *and* **ENOBARBUS** *enter.*

ANTONY

Promising favors? By Jove that thunders! Who are you, slave?

THIDIAS

A person who merely follows the orders of the best man, the man most worthy of service.

ENOBARBUS

You will be whipped.

ANTONY
    (calling for servants) Approach, there! *(to* THIDIAS*)* Ah, you
        kite!—Now, gods and devils!
    Authority melts from me. Of late, when I cried "Ho!"
    Like boys unto a muss kings would start forth
    And cry, "Your will?" *(calling to servants)* Have you no ears?
        I am
    Antony yet.

Enter a SERVANT, *followed by others*

                Take hence this jack and whip him.

ENOBARBUS
95   *(aside)* 'Tis better playing with a lion's whelp
    Than with an old one dying.

ANTONY
                  Moon and stars!
    Whip him. Were 't twenty of the greatest tributaries
    That do acknowledge Caesar, should I find them
    So saucy with the hand of she here—what's her name
100   Since she was Cleopatra? Whip him, fellows,
    Till like a boy, you see him cringe his face
    And whine aloud for mercy. Take him hence.

THIDIAS
    Mark Antony—

ANTONY
              Tug him away! Being whipped,
    Bring him again. This jack of Caesar's shall
105   Bear us an errand to him.
              Exeunt SERVANTS *with* THIDIAS
    (to CLEOPATRA*)* You were half blasted ere I knew you. Ha!
    Have I my pillow left unpressed in Rome,
    Forborne the getting of a lawful race,
    And by a gem of women, to be abused
110   By one that looks on feeders?

ANTONY

(calling for servants) Come here! *(to* THIDIAS*)* Ah, you bird of prey! Now by all the gods and devils, my authority weakens. Not long ago, when I cried, "Ho!" kings would jump up and cry, "What's your pleasure?" *(calling to servants)* Are you deaf? I'm still Antony.

A SERVANT *enters, followed by others.*

Take away this lout and whip him.

ENOBARBUS

(aside) It's safer to toy with a lion cub than an old, dying lion.

ANTONY

By the moon and stars! Whip him! If I saw twenty of the greatest powers that pay tribute to Caesar taking such liberties with her hand—what's her name now? This woman who once was Cleopatra, but now has become something different? Whip him, fellows, until he screws up his face like a baby and cries aloud for mercy! Take him away.

THIDIAS

Mark Antony—

ANTONY

Pull him away, and once he has been whipped, bring him back. Caesar's knave will bring him a message for us.

The SERVANTS *exit with* THIDIAS.

(to CLEOPATRA*)* You were damaged goods before I met you. Ha! Did I desert my bed in Rome, passing up the chance to have a legitimate family with a jewel of a woman, in order to be deceived by one who wastes her favors on servants?

CLEOPATRA
          Good my lord—

ANTONY
You have been a boggler ever.
But when we in our viciousness grow hard—
Oh, misery on 't!—the wise gods seel our eyes,
In our own filth drop our clear judgments, make us
115 Adore our errors, laugh at 's while we strut
To our confusion.

CLEOPATRA
        Oh, is 't come to this?

ANTONY
I found you as a morsel cold upon
Dead Caesar's trencher. Nay, you were a fragment
Of Gneius Pompey's, besides what hotter hours,
120 Unregistered in vulgar fame, you have
Luxuriously picked out. For I am sure,
Though you can guess what temperance should be,
You know not what it is.

CLEOPATRA
        Wherefore is this?

ANTONY
To let a fellow that will take rewards
125 And say "God quit you!" be familiar with
My playfellow, your hand, this kingly seal
And plighter of high hearts! Oh, that I were
Upon the hill of Basan, to outroar
The hornèd herd! For I have savage cause,
130 And to proclaim it civilly were like
A haltered neck which does the hangman thank
For being yare about him.

Enter a SERVANT *with* THIDIAS

        Is he whipped?

CLEOPATRA

My good lord—

ANTONY

You've always been a liar. But when our vices become habits—Oh, the sadness of it!—the wise gods blind us, shade our better judgment, make us love our mistakes, and laugh as we strut to our ruin.

CLEOPATRA

Oh, has it come to this?

ANTONY

You were a cold crumb on dead Julius Caesar's plate when I met you. No, you were one of Gneius Pompey's leftovers—not to mention your other, more depraved affairs, which have somehow managed to avoid becoming the subject of vulgar gossip. For I'm sure that although you may know what temperance is, you've never experienced it firsthand.

CLEOPATRA

Why are you doing this?

ANTONY

To let a servant be familiar with my little toy, your hand—a hand that has signed royal treaties and pledged your love to me—oh, if only I were standing on the hill of Basan, so that I could roar louder than that horned herd! For I have been savagely abused, and to state my grievances politely would be as absurd as a condemned criminal thanking the hangman for doing his job quickly.

Basan = home to herds of bulls (traditional symbols of men with adulterous wives), according to the Bible

A SERVANT *enters with* THIDIAS.

Has he been whipped?

SERVANT
Soundly, my lord.

ANTONY
Cried he? And begged he pardon?

SERVANT
135   He did ask favor.

ANTONY
(to THIDIAS*)* If that thy father live, let him repent
Thou wast not made his daughter, and be thou sorry
To follow Caesar in his triumph, since
Thou hast been whipped for following him. Henceforth
140   The white hand of a lady fever thee;
Shake thou to look on 't. Get thee back to Caesar.
Tell him thy entertainment. Look thou say
He makes me angry with him, for he seems
Proud and disdainful, harping on what I am,
145   Not what he knew I was. He makes me angry,
And at this time most easy 'tis to do 't,
When my good stars, that were my former guides,
Have empty left their orbs and shot their fires
Into th' abysm of hell. If he mislike
150   My speech and what is done, tell him he has
Hipparchus, my enfranchèd bondman, whom
He may at pleasure whip, or hang, or torture,
As he shall like, to quit me. Urge it thou.
Hence with thy stripes, begone!

Exit THIDIAS

CLEOPATRA
Have you done yet?

ANTONY
155   Alack, our terrene moon is now eclipsed,
And it portends alone the fall of Antony.

CLEOPATRA
(aside) I must stay his time.

SERVANT

Soundly, my lord.

ANTONY

Did he cry? Did he beg my pardon?

SERVANT

He did ask for mercy.

ANTONY

(to THIDIAS*)* If your father is alive, let him be sorry you weren't born a daughter. And you should be sorry to follow Caesar in his triumphal parade, since you have been whipped for following him. From now on, you should tremble and grow feverish whenever you see the white hand of a lady. Get yourself back to Caesar. Tell him how you've been treated. Be sure you tell him he makes me angry with him, because he seems proud and disdainful, harping on what I am now rather than what he knows. He makes me angry—and that's easy to do right now, now that my lucky stars have abandoned me. If he doesn't like what I've said or done, remind him that he holds Hipparchus, a slave I freed. He may whip, or hang, or torture him as he pleases. Then we will be even. Recommend that to him. Take your whipping scars and go.

THIDIAS *exits.*

CLEOPATRA

Are you done yet?

ANTONY

You, my earthly moon, are now eclipsed, and that alone foretells my ruin.

CLEOPATRA

(aside) I must wait for him to finish his tirade.

ANTONY
To flatter Caesar, would you mingle eyes
With one that ties his points?

CLEOPATRA

Not know me yet?

ANTONY
160   Coldhearted toward me?

CLEOPATRA

Ah, dear, if I be so,
From my cold heart let heaven engender hail,
And poison it in the source, and the first stone
Drop in my neck. As it determines, so
Dissolve my life! The next Caesarion smite,
165   Till by degrees the memory of my womb,
Together with my brave Egyptians all,
By the discandying of this pelleted storm
Lie graveless till the flies and gnats of Nile
Have buried them for prey!

ANTONY

I am satisfied.
170   Caesar sits down in Alexandria, where
I will oppose his fate. Our force by land
Hath nobly held. Our severed navy too
Have knit again, and fleet, threat'ning most sealike.
Where hast thou been, my heart? Dost thou hear, lady?
175   If from the field I shall return once more
To kiss these lips, I will appear in blood.
I and my sword will earn our chronicle.
There's hope in 't yet.

CLEOPATRA
That's my brave lord!

ANTONY
180   I will be treble-sinewed, -hearted, -breathed,
And fight maliciously. For when mine hours
Were nice and lucky, men did ransom lives
Of me for jests; but now I'll set my teeth

ANTONY

In order to flatter Caesar, would you flirt with the servant who laces up his pants?

CLEOPATRA

Don't you know me still?

ANTONY

Has your heart cooled toward me?

CLEOPATRA

Ah, dear, if that is true, let heaven make poisonous hail grow from my heart, and let the first hailstone drop down my throat. As it dissolves, so shall my life. The next hailstone should hit Caesarion, until one by one all my children, and every one of my brave Egyptians, are killed by the dissolving of this pellet storm and lie unburied, covered by gnats and flies.

ANTONY

I am satisfied. Caesar has made camp in Alexandria. I will fight him there. Our land forces have bravely stood firm. Our tattered navy has reassembled and set sail, as formidable as the sea itself. Where have you been, my bravery? Do you hear what I say, lady? If I come back from the battlefield again to kiss those lips, I'll be covered in blood. My sword and I will earn our place in history. We still have hope.

CLEOPATRA

That's my brave lord!

ANTONY

I'll be triple the soldier I was in strength, bravery, and stamina. I'll fight brutally. In the days when I had better luck, prisoners of war could buy their freedoms from me with simple trinkets. But now I'll grit my

And send to darkness all that stop me. Come,
185 Let's have one other gaudy night. Call to me
All my sad captains. Fill our bowls once more.
Let's mock the midnight bell.

CLEOPATRA
                                It is my birthday.
I had thought t' have held it poor; but since my lord
Is Antony again, I will be Cleopatra.

ANTONY
190 We will yet do well.

CLEOPATRA
(to ENOBARBUS) Call all his noble captains to my lord.

ANTONY
Do so. We'll speak to them, and tonight I'll force
The wine peep through their scars.—Come on, my Queen,
There's sap in 't yet. The next time I do fight
195 I'll make Death love me, for I will contend
Even with his pestilent scythe.
                                Exeunt all but ENOBARBUS

ENOBARBUS
Now he'll outstare the lightning. To be furious
Is to be frighted out of fear, and in that mood
The dove will peck the estridge; and I see still
200 A diminution in our captain's brain
Restores his heart. When valor preys on reason,
It eats the sword it fights with. I will seek
Some way to leave him.
                                            Exit

teeth and kill anyone who tries to stop me. Come, let's have one more extravagant night. Invite all my sad captains. Fill our wine bowls again. Let's drink through midnight.

CLEOPATRA

It's my birthday. I had planned to celebrate it quietly, but since my lord is once more himself, I will be Cleopatra again.

ANTONY

We'll win yet.

CLEOPATRA

(to ENOBARBUS*)* Call all my lord's noble captains to him.

ANTONY

Do so. I'll speak to them, and then tonight I'll get them all so drunk that the wine seeps out of their old war wounds. Come on, my Queen. There's still life in our cause. The next time I fight, I'll make Death love me. I'll compete even with his fatal scythe.

> *Everyone except* ENOBARBUS *exits.*

ENOBARBUS

Now he'll work himself up to a fury. Rage scares away a man's fear. In that state, a dove will attack an ostrich. I have always noticed that when my captain's reason is diminished, his bravery increases. When courage consumes reason, it destroys its only weapon. I'll look for some way to leave his service.

> *He exits.*

ACT FOUR

SCENE 1

Enter CAESAR, AGRIPPA, *and* MAECENAS, *with his army,*
CAESAR *reading a letter*

CAESAR
    He calls me "boy" and chides as he had power
    To beat me out of Egypt. My messenger
    He hath whipped with rods, dares me to personal combat,
    Caesar to Antony. Let the old ruffian know
5   I have many other ways to die, meantime
    Laugh at his challenge.

MAECENAS
                Caesar must think
    When one so great begins to rage, he's hunted
    Even to falling. Give him no breath, but now
10   Make boot of his distraction. Never anger
    Made good guard for itself.

CAESAR
                        Let our best heads
    Know that tomorrow the last of many battles
    We mean to fight. Within our files there are,
    Of those that served Mark Antony but late,
15   Enough to fetch him in. See it done
    And feast the army. We have store to do 't,
    And they have earned the waste. Poor Antony!

                                       Exeunt

ACT FOUR

SCENE 1

CAESAR *enters, reading a letter, with* AGRIPPA, MAECENAS, *and his army.*

CAESAR

He calls me "boy" and scolds me as if he had the power to whip me out of Egypt. He whipped my messenger with rods. He dares me to personal combat, Caesar against Antony. Let the old ruffian discover that I have many other ways to die, and in the meantime, we'll laugh at his challenge.

MAECENAS

Caesar must realize that when a man as powerful as Antony begins to rage, he has been pursued to the point of collapse. Don't give him time to catch his breath. Take advantage of his unreasonable rage. Anger does not protect the angry well.

CAESAR

Tell our top commanders that I want tomorrow's battle to be the last we fight. Our army has recently acquired many of Mark Antony's former soldiers—enough to capture him. See that it is done, and prepare a feast for the soldiers. We have enough supplies for it, and they've earned it. Poor Antony!

They exit.

ACT 4, SCENE 2

Enter ANTONY, CLEOPATRA, ENOBARBUS, CHARMIAN, *and*
IRAS, *with others*

ANTONY
He will not fight with me, Domitius?

ENOBARBUS
                                                    No.

ANTONY
Why should he not?

ENOBARBUS
He thinks, being twenty times of better fortune,
He is twenty men to one.

ANTONY
                                        Tomorrow, soldier,
5   By sea and land I'll fight. Or I will live
Or bathe my dying honor in the blood
Shall make it live again. Woo't thou fight well?

ENOBARBUS
I'll strike and cry, "Take all."

ANTONY
                                        Well said. Come on!
Call forth my household servants.

Enter three or four SERVITORS

                                        Let's tonight
10 Be bounteous at our meal.

Greeting them one by one

                                        Give me thy hand.
Thou hast been rightly honest.—So hast thou,—

ACT 4, SCENE 2

ANTONY, CLEOPATRA, ENOBARBUS, CHARMIAN, *and*
IRAS *enter, with attendants.*

ANTONY

He won't fight with me, Domitius?

ENOBARBUS

No.

ANTONY

Why won't he?

ENOBARBUS

He thinks that since his fortune is twenty times better
than yours, it would be like pitting twenty men
against one.

ANTONY

Tomorrow, soldier, I'll fight by sea and land. By the
end I will either live, or else I'll restore my honor by
shedding my blood. Will you fight well?

ENOBARBUS

When I strike, I'll cry, "All or nothing!"

ANTONY

Well put. Come on. Call out my household servants.

Three or four SERVANTS *enter.*

Tonight let's have plenty to eat.

He greets the SERVANTS *one by one.*

Give me your hand; you've been truly honest—so have
you and you—and you—you too.

Thou,—and thou,—and thou. You have served me well,
And kings have been your fellows.

CLEOPATRA

(aside to ENOBARBUS*)* What means this?

ENOBARBUS

15   *(aside to* CLEOPATRA*)* 'Tis one of those odd tricks which
        sorrow shoots
Out of the mind.

ANTONY

            (to another SERVITOR*)* And thou art honest too.
I wish I could be made so many men,
And all of you clapped up together in
An Antony, that I might do you service
20   So good as you have done.

ALL THE SERVITORS

                        The gods forbid!

ANTONY

Well, my good fellows, wait on me tonight.
Scant not my cups, and make as much of me
As when mine empire was your fellow too,
And suffered my command.

CLEOPATRA

25   *(aside to* ENOBARBUS*)* What does he mean?

ENOBARBUS

(aside to CLEOPATRA*)* To make his followers weep.

ANTONY

(to the SERVITORS*)* Tend me tonight.
May be it is the period of your duty.
Haply you shall not see me more, or if,
30   A mangled shadow. Perchance tomorrow
You'll serve another master. I look on you
As one that takes his leave. Mine honest friends,
I turn you not away, but, like a master
Married to your good service, stay till death.
35   Tend me tonight two hours, I ask no more,
And the gods yield you for 't!

You have all served me well, and kings are your peers.

CLEOPATRA

(aside to ENOBARBUS*)* What is this?

ENOBARBUS

(aside to CLEOPATRA*)* It's one of those nostalgic moods caused by sorrow.

ANTONY

(to another SERVANT*)* And you're honest too. I wish I could split into as many men as there are servants here before me, and that all of you could merge into a single Antony, so I could give you the same good service you've given me.

ALL THE SERVANTS

The gods forbid!

ANTONY

Well, my good fellows, wait on me tonight. Keep my cups full and treat me as you did when my empire was one of your fellow servants, obeying my commands.

CLEOPATRA

(to ENOBARBUS*)* Why is he doing this?

ENOBARBUS

(to CLEOPATRA*)* He wants to make his followers weep.

ANTONY

(to the SERVANTS*)* Wait on me tonight. It's possible that this will be the end of your service. It's possible you won't see me again, or if you do, it will only be my mangled body. Perhaps tomorrow you'll be serving another master. I look upon you as a person saying good-bye. My honest friends, I won't turn you away, but like a master dependent on your good service, I will stay with you until death separates us. Serve me tonight for two hours—I don't ask any more—and may the gods bless you for it.

ENOBARBUS
                              What mean you, sir,
To give them this discomfort? Look, they weep,
And I, an ass, am onion-eyed. For shame,
Transform us not to women.

ANTONY
                              Ho, ho, ho!
40 Now the witch take me if I meant it thus!
Grace grow where those drops fall! My hearty friends,
You take me in too dolorous a sense,
For I spake to you for your comfort, did desire you
To burn this night with torches. Know, my hearts,
45 I hope well of tomorrow, and will lead you
Where rather I'll expect victorious life
Than death and honor. Let's to supper, come,
And drown consideration.

                                        Exeunt

ENOBARBUS

> What are you doing, sir? You're making them uncomfortable. Look—they're crying. And I'm just foolish enough to tear up myself. It's embarrassing. Don't turn us into women.

ANTONY

> Ha, ha, ha! May the evil one take me if I meant it like that! Those tears will bring blessings to you. You interpret my words in a melancholy sense, my hearty friends. I spoke to encourage you, asking that you help me make this night a brilliant one. You should know, my friends, that I have good hopes for tomorrow, and that I will lead you as if I expect victory rather than an honorable death. Let's go to supper. Come, and let's drown our worries.

> *They exit.*

ACT 4, SCENE 3

Enter a company of SOLDIERS

FIRST SOLDIER
Brother, good night. Tomorrow is the day.

SECOND SOLDIER
It will determine one way. Fare you well.
Heard you of nothing strange about the streets?

FIRST SOLDIER
Nothing. What news?

SECOND SOLDIER
5   Belike 'tis but a rumor. Good night to you.

FIRST SOLDIER
Well, sir, good night.

They meet other SOLDIERS

SECOND SOLDIER
Soldiers, have careful watch.

THIRD SOLDIER
And you. Good night, good night.

The four SOLDIERS *place themselves in every corner of the stage*

SECOND SOLDIER
Here we. And if tomorrow
10   Our navy thrive, I have an absolute hope
Our landmen will stand up.

FIRST SOLDIER
'Tis a brave army, and full of purpose.

Music of the hautboys is under the stage

ACT 4, SCENE 3

A company of SOLDIERS *enters.*

FIRST SOLDIER
Good night, brother. Tomorrow is the day.

SECOND SOLDIER
This battle will determine who wins the war. Take care of yourself. Have you heard about anything unusual happening in the city?

FIRST SOLDIER
No. What was it?

SECOND SOLDIER
It was probably just a rumor. Good night.

FIRST SOLDIER
Well sir, good night.

Two other SOLDIERS *enter.*

SECOND SOLDIER
Soldiers, watch carefully.

THIRD SOLDIER
You too. Good night. Good night.

Each SOLDIER *takes a post at a corner of the stage.*

SECOND SOLDIER
This is our station. And if our navy wins tomorrow, no doubt our army will do their part.

FIRST SOLDIER
It's an outstanding army and highly motivated.

Oboe music comes from underneath the stage.

SECOND SOLDIER
Peace! What noise?

FIRST SOLDIER
List, list!

SECOND SOLDIER
15   Hark!

FIRST SOLDIER
Music i' th' air.

THIRD SOLDIER
Under the earth.

FOURTH SOLDIER
It signs well, does it not?

THIRD SOLDIER
No.

FIRST SOLDIER
20   Peace, I say! What should this mean?

SECOND SOLDIER
'Tis the god Hercules, whom Antony loved,
Now leaves him.

FIRST SOLDIER
Walk. Let's see if other watchmen
Do hear what we do.

They advance toward the other SOLDIERS

SECOND SOLDIER
25   How now, masters?

ALL
(speak together) How now? How now? Do you hear this?

FIRST SOLDIER
Ay. Is 't not strange?

THIRD SOLDIER
Do you hear, masters? Do you hear?

SECOND SOLDIER
> Quiet! What's that sound?

FIRST SOLDIER
> Listen! Listen!

SECOND SOLDIER
> Listen!

FIRST SOLDIER
> There's music coming out of thin air.

THIRD SOLDIER
> From under the earth.

FOURTH SOLDIER
> It's a lucky sign, isn't it?

THIRD SOLDIER
> No.

FIRST SOLDIER
> Quiet, I say. What does this mean?

SECOND SOLDIER

Antony's family claimed to be descended from the demigod Hercules.

> It means that Antony's patron god, Hercules, is leaving him.

FIRST SOLDIER
> Let's walk over and see if the other soldiers heard the same thing.

They go to speak with the other SOLDIERS.

SECOND SOLDIER
> Hello there, good sirs.

ALL
> *(speaking at the same time)* What now? What now? Do you hear that?

FIRST SOLDIER
> Yes. Isn't it strange?

THIRD SOLDIER
> Do you hear that, men? Do you?

FIRST SOLDIER
Follow the noise so far as we have quarter;
30   Let's see how it will give off.

ALL
                                    Content. 'Tis strange.
                                                    Exeunt

FIRST SOLDIER

Let's follow the music as far as we can without leaving our station and see if it stops.

ALL

Good idea. It's very strange.

They exit.

ACT 4, SCENE 4

Enter ANTONY *and* CLEOPATRA, *with* CHARMIAN *and others attending*

ANTONY
(calling) Eros! Mine armor, Eros!

CLEOPATRA
                                        Sleep a little.

ANTONY
No, my chuck.—Eros, come, mine armor, Eros!

Enter EROS *with armor*

Come, good fellow, put thine iron on.
If fortune be not ours today, it is
Because we brave her. Come.

CLEOPATRA
                                        Nay, I'll help too.
What's this for?

She helps to arm him

ANTONY
                                        Ah, let be, let be! Thou art
The armorer of my heart. False, false. This, this.

CLEOPATRA
Sooth, la, I'll help. Thus it must be.

ANTONY
                                                Well, well,
We shall thrive now.—Seest thou, my good fellow?
Go put on thy defenses.

EROS
                                        Briefly, sir.

CLEOPATRA
Is not this buckled well?

ACT 4, SCENE 4

ANTONY and CLEOPATRA *enter with* CHARMIAN *and others of the court.*

ANTONY

(calling) Eros! Bring my armor, Eros.

CLEOPATRA

Get a little sleep.

ANTONY

No, my dear . . . Eros, come on, bring my armor, Eros.

EROS *enters, carrying* ANTONY*'s armor.*

Come on, good fellow, help me into that armor you're carrying. If luck deserts us today, it's because we defy it. Come on.

CLEOPATRA

No, I'll help too. What's this part for?

She picks up a piece of the armor.

ANTONY

Ah, leave it alone. Leave it alone! You armor my heart. No! No! That part goes there.

CLEOPATRA

Really, I'll help. It must go like this.

ANTONY

Yes, well done. We've got it now.—Do you see this, my good fellow? Go and put on your own armor.

EROS

In a minute, sir.

CLEOPATRA

Didn't I buckle this well?

ANTONY
                    Rarely, rarely.
He that unbuckles this, till we do please
To doff 't for our repose, shall hear a storm.—
Thou fumblest, Eros, and my Queen's a squire
15   More tight at this than thou. Dispatch.—O love,
That thou couldst see my wars today, and knew'st
The royal occupation! Thou shouldst see
A workman in 't.

Enter an armed SOLDIER

                    Good morrow to thee. Welcome.
Thou look'st like him that knows a warlike charge.
20   To business that we love we rise betimes
And go to 't with delight.

SOLDIER
                    A thousand, sir,
Early though 't be, have on their riveted trim
And at the port expect you.

Shout. Trumpets flourish

Enter CAPTAINS *and* SOLDIERS

CAPTAIN
    The morn is fair. Good morrow, General.

ALL
25   Good morrow, General.

ANTONY
                    'Tis well blown, lads.
This morning, like the spirit of a youth
That means to be of note, begins betimes.
So, so. *(to* CLEOPATRA*)* Come, give me that. This way. Well
            said.
Fare thee well, dame.

ANTONY

Excellently, excellently. Anyone who unbuckles this before I want to take it off to rest will be sorry.— You're fumbling, Eros. My Queen's a better squire than you are. Hurry.—Oh, love, if you could only watch the battle today and see how expert I am at my craft.

An armed SOLDIER *enters.*

Good morning to you. Welcome. You look like a person who knows the business of war. When we love our job we get up early and go to it joyfully.

SOLDIER

Even though it's early, there are already a thousand armored soldiers waiting for you at the harbor.

A shout is heard, then a trumpet fanfare. CAPTAINS *and* SOLDIERS *enter.*

CAPTAIN

The weather is fair. Good morning, General.

ALL

Good morning, General.

ANTONY

That was a fine fanfare, boys. Like a young man who wants to amount to something, this morning begins early. *(to* CLEOPATRA*)* So, so. Here, give me that. This is how it goes on. Well done.

Farewell, lady.

He kisses her

                                    Whate'er becomes of me,

30   This is a soldier's kiss. Rebukable
And worthy shameful check it were to stand
On more mechanic compliment. I'll leave thee
Now like a man of steel. *(to others)* You that will fight,
Follow me close. I'll bring you to 't. *(to* CLEOPATRA*)* Adieu.
                Exeunt ANTONY, EROS, CAPTAINS,
                            and SOLDIERS

CHARMIAN
35   Please you retire to your chamber?

CLEOPATRA
                          Lead me.
He goes forth gallantly. That he and Caesar might
Determine this great war in single fight!
Then Antony—but now—. Well, on.
                                      Exeunt

He kisses her.

Whatever happens to me, this is a soldier's kiss. It would be shameful to draw out our good-byes. I'll leave you without revealing any emotion, like a man of steel. *(to the others)* Anyone who wants to fight, follow me now, and I'll see you get your wish. *(to* CLEOPATRA*)* Good-bye.

> ANTONY *and* EROS *exit with the*
> CAPTAINS *and* SOLDIERS.

CHARMIAN

If it pleases you, let's go to your room.

CLEOPATRA

Lead the way. He goes forth to war bravely. If only he and Caesar could determine the outcome of this war by single combat! Then Antony would—but, with circumstances as they are—well, let's go.

> *They exit.*

ACT 4, SCENE 5

Trumpets sound. Enter ANTONY *and* EROS, *and a* SOLDIER *meeting them*

SOLDIER
The gods make this a happy day to Antony!

ANTONY
Would thou and those thy scars had once prevailed
To make me fight at land!

SOLDIER
                              Hadst thou done so,
The kings that have revolted, and the soldier
That has this morning left thee, would have still
Followed thy heels.

ANTONY
                    Who's gone this morning?

SOLDIER
                                        Who?
One ever near thee. Call for Enobarbus
He shall not hear thee, or from Caesar's camp
Say "I am none of thine."

ANTONY
                    What sayest thou?

SOLDIER
                                        Sir,
He is with Caesar.

EROS
                    Sir, his chests and treasure
He has not with him.

ANTONY
                Is he gone?

SOLDIER
                          Most certain.

ACT 4, SCENE 5

Trumpets sound. ANTONY *and* EROS *enter and are met by a* SOLDIER *entering from another direction.*

SOLDIER

May the gods bless Antony today!

ANTONY

I wish you and your scarred self had convinced me to wage our last battle on land.

SOLDIER

If you had, the kings that have revolted and the soldier that deserted this morning would still be behind you.

ANTONY

Who deserted this morning?

SOLDIER

You don't know? Someone who was always near you. If you call for Enobarbus, he won't hear you. Or if he can hear you from Caesar's camp, he'll reply, "I'm no longer on your side."

ANTONY

What are you saying?

SOLDIER

Sir, he's with Caesar.

EROS

Sir, he left his belongings and treasure.

ANTONY

He's gone?

SOLDIER

It's certain.

ANTONY
  Go, Eros, send his treasure after. Do it.
  Detain no jot, I charge thee. Write to him—
  I will subscribe—gentle adieus and greetings.
15 Say that I wish he never find more cause
  To change a master. Oh, my fortunes have
  Corrupted honest men! Dispatch.—Enobarbus!

                                                     Exeunt

ANTONY

Eros, send his treasure to him. Do it now. Don't keep anything back, I insist. Write to him from me—I'll sign it—sending greetings and gentle good-byes. Say that I hope he never has cause to look for a new master. Oh, my bad luck has forced honest men to become traitors. Hurry. Enobarbus!

They exit.

ACT 4, SCENE 6

Flourish. Enter AGRIPPA, *and* CAESAR, *with* ENOBARBUS
and DOLABELLA

CAESAR
Go forth, Agrippa, and begin the fight.
Our will is Antony be took alive.
Make it so known.

AGRIPPA
Caesar, I shall.

Exit

CAESAR
5   The time of universal peace is near.
Prove this a prosp'rous day, the three-nooked world
Shall bear the olive freely.

Enter a MESSENGER

MESSENGER
                              Antony
Is come into the field.

CAESAR
                              Go charge Agrippa
Plant those that have revolted in the vant,
10   That Antony may seem to spend his fury
Upon himself.

Exeunt all but ENOBARBUS

ENOBARBUS
Alexas did revolt and went to Jewry on
Affairs of Antony, there did dissuade
Great Herod to incline himself to Caesar
15   And leave his master Antony. For this pains
Caesar hath hanged him. Canidius and the rest
That fell away have entertainment but
No honorable trust. I have done ill,

ACT 4, SCENE 6

Trumpet fanfare. AGRIPPA *and* CAESAR *enter with*
ENOBARBUS *and* DOLABELLA.

CAESAR

Agrippa, go start the battle. We want Antony taken
alive. Make sure everyone knows that.

AGRIPPA

I will, Caesar.

He exits.

CAESAR

An era of universal peace is about to start. If this battle
goes well for us, there will be peace in all three corners
of the world.

the three corners
of the world =
Africa, Asia, and
Europe, which
were all under
Roman rule

A MESSENGER *enters.*

MESSENGER

Antony has come onto the battlefield.

CAESAR

Go order Agrippa to put the men who deserted
Antony's army at the front. That way Antony will
feel like he's fighting his own men.

Everyone exits except ENOBARBUS.

ENOBARBUS

Alexas deserted. He went to Judea as if on Antony's
business, but he persuaded Herod to support Caesar
instead. Caesar hanged him for this service. Canidius
and the others that left Antony are given hospitality
here but no positions of trust. I've done a bad thing,

20   Of which I do accuse myself so sorely
      That I will joy no more.

      Enter a SOLDIER *of Caesar's*

SOLDIER
                          Enobarbus, Antony
      Hath after thee sent all thy treasure, with
      His bounty overplus. The messenger
      Came on my guard, and at thy tent is now
      Unloading of his mules.

ENOBARBUS
25   I give it you.

SOLDIER
      Mock not, Enobarbus.
      I tell you true. Best you safed the bringer
      Out of the host. I must attend mine office,
      Or would have done 't myself. Your Emperor
30   Continues still a Jove.

                                              Exit

ENOBARBUS
      I am alone the villain of the earth,
      And feel I am so most. O Antony,
      Thou mine of bounty, how wouldst thou have paid
      My better service, when my turpitude
35   Thou dost so crown with gold! This blows my heart.
      If swift thought break it not, a swifter mean
      Shall outstrike thought, but thought will do 't, I feel.
      I fight against thee? No, I will go seek
      Some ditch wherein to die. The foul'st best fits
40   My latter part of life.

                                              Exit

for which I will blame myself so much that I'll never be happy again.

A SOLDIER *of Caesar's enters.*

SOLDIER

Enobarbus, Antony has sent you all your treasure, with generous gifts besides. The messenger arrived on my watch and is unloading his mules at your tent.

ENOBARBUS

It's yours.

SOLDIER

Don't joke about this, Enobarbus. I'm telling you the truth. You'd better bring the messenger safely through the lines so he can return. I'd do it myself, but I can't leave my post. Your Emperor is still a king among gods.

He exits.

ENOBARBUS

I am the worst person alive, and I know it the best. Oh, Antony, you extravagantly generous man, how would you have rewarded me for serving you faithfully when you reward my badness with all of this gold! My heart feels like it's about to explode. If grief doesn't kill me, I'll find a quicker way to kill myself—even though I think grief will do the job just as well. I, fight against you, Antony? No, I'll go find some ditch to die in. The foulest fate would be most appropriate for me now in this latest phase of my life.

He exits.

ACT 4, SCENE 7

Alarum. Drums and trumpets. Enter AGRIPPA *and others*

AGRIPPA
Retire! We have engaged ourselves too far.
Caesar himself has work, and our oppression
Exceeds what we expected.

Exeunt

Alarums. Enter ANTONY, *and* SCARUS, *wounded*

SCARUS
O my brave Emperor, this is fought indeed!
5   Had we done so at first, we had droven them home
With clouts about their heads.

ANTONY
                                                        Thou bleed'st apace.

SCARUS
I had a wound here that was like a "T,"
But now 'tis made an "H."

Sound retreat far off

ANTONY
                                                        They do retire.

SCARUS
We'll beat 'em into bench-holes. I have yet
10   Room for six scotches more.

Enter EROS

EROS
They are beaten, sir, and our advantage serves
For a fair victory.

ACT 4, SCENE 7

A call to battle is sounded. Drums and trumpets sound.
AGRIPPA *and other soldiers of Caesar's enter.*

AGRIPPA

Retreat! We've advanced too far. Caesar himself is in trouble and there are more adversaries than we expected.

They exit.

A battle call. ANTONY *enters with* SCARUS,
who is wounded.

SCARUS

Oh, my brave Emperor, this is what I call a fight! If we'd fought like this before, we'd have driven them home with bandaged heads.

ANTONY

You're bleeding a lot.

SCARUS

I had a scar here that looked like a "T"; now it's an "H."

Distant trumpets sound the retreat.

ANTONY

They're retreating.

SCARUS

We'll chase 'em into their latrines. I still have room for six more wounds.

EROS *enters.*

EROS

They're retreating, sir, and our superiority indicates a clear victory.

SCARUS
                        Let us score their backs
And snatch 'em up, as we take hares, behind!
'Tis sport to maul a runner.

ANTONY
                              I will reward thee
15   Once for thy sprightly comfort and tenfold
For thy good valor. Come thee on.

SCARUS
                              I'll halt after.

                                        Exeunt

SCARUS

Let's slash their backs and grab 'em like we do rabbits, from behind. It's fair game to mark a coward.

ANTONY

I'll reward you once for your cheerfulness and ten times for your courage. Come on.

SCARUS

I'll limp after you.

They exit.

ACT 4, SCENE 8

Alarum. Enter ANTONY *again in a march;* SCARUS, *with others*

ANTONY
We have beat him to his camp. Run one before
And let the Queen know of our gests.

Exit a soldier
                                        Tomorrow,
Before the sun shall see 's, we'll spill the blood
That has today escaped. I thank you all,
5   For doughty-handed are you, and have fought
Not as you served the cause, but as 't had been
Each man's like mine. You have shown all Hectors.
Enter the city. Clip your wives, your friends.
Tell them your feats, whilst they with joyful tears
10   Wash the congealment from your wounds and kiss
The honored gashes whole.

Enter CLEOPATRA

(to SCARUS*)*   Give me thy hand.
To this great fairy I'll commend thy acts,
Make her thanks bless thee. O thou day o' the world,
(to CLEOPATRA*)* Chain mine armed neck. Leap thou, attire
          and all,
15   Through proof of harness to my heart, and there
Ride on the pants triumphing!

CLEOPATRA
                                        Lord of lords!
O infinite virtue, com'st thou smiling from
The world's great snare uncaught?

ANTONY
                                        Mine nightingale,
We have beat them to their beds. What, girl, though gray

ACT 4, SCENE 8

A battle call. ANTONY *marches in, followed by* SCARUS *and others.*

ANTONY

We've driven him all the way back to his camp. One of you run to the Queen with the news.

A soldier exits.

Before sunrise tomorrow, we'll kill anyone who escaped today. I want to thank all of you. You're formidable. You fought not as if you served the cause but as though it were as much your personal fight as mine. You are all Hectors. Go on into the city. Embrace your wives and your friends. Describe your feats for them while they cry for joy. Their tears will wash the congealed blood from your wounds, and they will kiss those honorable cuts until they heal.

Hector = powerful
Trojan warrior

CLEOPATRA *enters.*

(to SCARUS*)* Give me your hand. I'll praise your actions to this powerful enchantress so that she will thank you with blessings. Oh, light of the world, *(to* CLEOPATRA*)* wrap your arms around my armored neck. Leap, with all your finery through my armor and go straight to my heart. There you can ride upon my heartbeats, sharing in my triumph.

CLEOPATRA

Lord of lords! Your courage is infinite. Have you returned smiling from the great battle for the world?

ANTONY

My songbird, we have beaten them to their beds. What do you think, girl!

20 Do something mingle with our younger brown, yet ha' we
A brain that nourishes our nerves and can
Get goal for goal of youth. Behold this man.
Commend unto his lips thy favoring hand.
(to SCARUS*)* Kiss it, my warrior.

SCARUS *kisses* CLEOPATRA*'s hand*

                                        He hath fought today
25 As if a god, in hate of mankind, had
Destroyed in such a shape.

CLEOPATRA
        (to SCARUS*)*   I'll give thee, friend,
An armor all of gold. It was a king's.

ANTONY
He has deserved it, were it carbuncled
Like holy Phoebus' car. Give me thy hand.
30 Through Alexandria make a jolly march.
Bear our hacked targets like the men that owe them.
Had our great palace the capacity
To camp this host, we all would sup together
And drink carouses to the next day's fate,
35 Which promises royal peril.—Trumpeters,
With brazen din blast you the city's ear;
Make mingle with our rattling taborins,
That heaven and earth may strike their sounds together,
Applauding our approach.
                                        Exeunt

Even though there are some gray hairs among the brown, I still have a brain and muscles that will let me compete with younger men. Look at this man. Show him favor by letting him kiss your hand. *(to* SCARUS*)* Kiss it, my warrior.

SCARUS *kisses* CLEOPATRA*'s hand*

Today he fought as though he were a god who hated mankind.

CLEOPATRA

(to SCARUS*)* Friend, I'll give you armor made of gold. It belonged to a king.

ANTONY

He deserves it, even if it were covered with jewels like holy Phoebus' car. Give me your hand. Let's have a cheerful march through Alexandria, proudly carrying our dented shields. If we had enough room in the palace to house this army, we'd all eat together and toast tomorrow, which promises to be full of danger. Trumpeters, blast the city's ears. Mix your fanfares with our drums, so that sounds from both heaven and earth will herald our approach.

> Phoebus' car = the chariot that the sun god Phoebus drove across the sky

Everyone exits.

ACT 4, SCENE 9

Enter a SENTRY *and his company.* ENOBARBUS *follows*

SENTRY
    If we be not relieved within this hour,
    We must return to th' court of guard. The night
    Is shiny, and they say we shall embattle
    By th' second hour i' th' morn.

FIRST WATCH
5   This last day was a shrewd one to 's.

ENOBARBUS
    O bear me witness, night—

SECOND WATCH
    What man is this?

FIRST WATCH
    Stand close and list him.

ENOBARBUS
    Be witness to me, O thou blessèd moon,
10   When men revolted shall upon record
    Bear hateful memory, poor Enobarbus did
    Before thy face repent.

SENTRY
    Enobarbus?

SECOND WATCH
    Peace! Hark further.

ENOBARBUS
15   O sovereign mistress of true melancholy,
    The poisonous damp of night dísponge upon me,
    That life, a very rebel to my will,
    May hang no longer on me. Throw my heart
    Against the flint and hardness of my fault,
20   Which, being dried with grief, will break to powder
    And finish all foul thoughts. O Antony,
    Nobler than my revolt is infamous,

ACT 4, SCENE 9

A SENTRY *and his company enter, followed by*
ENOBARBUS.

SENTRY

If we aren't relieved in an hour, we have to return to
our barracks. The night is bright, and they say we'll be
forming for battle by two A.M.

FIRST WATCH
That last day was a hard one for us.

ENOBARBUS
Oh, listen to me, night—

SECOND WATCH
Who is this?

FIRST WATCH
Stay hidden and listen.

ENOBARBUS

Be my witness, oh you blessed moon. The men who
revolted against Antony will be remembered scorn-
fully in the history books. But poor Enobarbus
repented.

SENTRY

That's Enobarbus?

SECOND WATCH
Quiet! Keep listening.

ENOBARBUS

Oh, moon, you queen of sadness, drop poisonous dew
on me so that my life, which continues against my
wishes, will end. Take my heart and throw it against
my hard, stony sin. My heart, which dried out with
grief, will surely break apart into a powder, and that
will be the end of my disgusting mind. Oh, Antony!
You are more noble than my revolt is dishonorable.

Forgive me in thine own particular,
But let the world rank me in register
25   A master-leaver and a fugitive.
O Antony! O Antony!

He dies

FIRST WATCH
Let's speak to him.

SENTRY
Let's hear him, for the things he speaks may concern Caesar.

SECOND WATCH
Let's do so. But he sleeps.

SENTRY
30   Swoons rather, for so bad a prayer as his
Was never yet for sleep.

FIRST WATCH
Go we to him.

SECOND WATCH
Awake, sir, awake. Speak to us.

FIRST WATCH
Hear you, sir?

SENTRY
35   The hand of death hath raught him.

Drums afar off

Hark, the drums
Demurely wake the sleepers. Let us bear him
To th' court of guard. He is of note. Our hour
Is fully out.

SECOND WATCH
Come on, then. He may recover yet.

Exeunt with the body

Forgive my crimes against you, but let history record me as a fugitive traitor. Oh, Antony! Oh, Antony!

He dies.

FIRST WATCH
Let's speak to him.

SENTRY
Let's listen to him. He may say something concerning Caesar.

SECOND WATCH
Good idea. But he's sleeping.

SENTRY
It looks more like he fainted. No one ever gave a prayer like that before going to sleep.

FIRST WATCH
Let's go to him.

SECOND WATCH
Wake up, sir, wake up. Speak to us.

FIRST WATCH
Do you hear us, sir?

SENTRY
The hand of death has taken him.

Drums are heard in the distance.

Listen. The drums softly wake the sleepers. Let's carry him to the barracks. He's an important person. Our hour is up.

SECOND WATCH
Come on, then. He may recover yet.
They exit, carrying ENOBARBUS'S *body.*

ACT 4, SCENE 10

Enter ANTONY *and* SCARUS, *with their army*

ANTONY
>Their preparation is today by sea.
>We please them not by land.

SCARUS
>   For both, my lord.

ANTONY
>I would they'd fight i' th' fire or i' th' air,
>We'd fight there too. But this it is: our foot
5 >Upon the hills adjoining to the city
>Shall stay with us. Order for sea is given;
>They have put forth the haven,
>Where their appointment we may best discover
>And look on their endeavor.

>   *Exeunt*

ACT 4, SCENE 10

ANTONY *and* SCARUS *enter, with the army.*

ANTONY

They've switched their operation to the sea today. We
didn't please them on land.

SCARUS

We're ready for both, my lord.

ANTONY

I wish they'd fight in fire or in the air. We'd meet them
there too. But here's the plan: our army will stay with
us on the hills by the city. Orders have been given to
the navy and they've left port. We'll be able to analyze
and direct the battle better from the hills.

They exit.

ACT 4, SCENE 11

Enter CAESAR *and his army*

CAESAR
But being charged, we will be still by land—
Which, as I take 't, we shall, for his best force
Is forth to man his galleys. To the vales,
And hold our best advantage.

Exeunt

ACT 4, SCENE 11

CAESAR *and his army enter.*

CAESAR

We won't move our land forces unless we're attacked. And I doubt that will happen, since most of Antony's men are with his navy. Let's take up the best positions we can in the valleys.

They exit.

ACT 4, SCENE 12

Enter ANTONY *and* SCARUS

ANTONY
    Yet they are not joined. Where yond pine does stand
    I shall discover all. I'll bring thee word
    Straight how 'tis like to go.

                                Exit

Alarum afar off, as at a sea fight

SCARUS
                       Swallows have built
    In Cleopatra's sails their nests. The auguries
5   Say they know not, they cannot tell, look grimly,
    And dare not speak their knowledge. Antony
    Is valiant and dejected, and by starts
    His fretted fortunes give him hope and fear
    Of what he has and has not.

Enter ANTONY

ANTONY
                     All is lost!
10   This foul Egyptian hath betrayèd me.
    My fleet hath yielded to the foe, and yonder
    They cast their caps up and carouse together
    Like friends long lost. Triple-turned whore! 'Tis thou
    Hast sold me to this novice, and my heart
15   Makes only wars on thee. Bid them all fly,
    For when I am revenged upon my charm,
    I have done all. Bid them all fly. Begone!

                            Exit SCARUS

    O sun, thy uprise shall I see no more.
    Fortune and Antony part here. Even here
20   Do we shake hands. All come to this? The hearts

ACT 4, SCENE 12

ANTONY *and* SCARUS *enter.*

ANTONY

They still haven't joined the battle. I'll be able to see better from that pine tree over there. I'll let you know right away how it's going.

> *He exits.*
> *Noises like a sea battle are heard in the distance.*

SCARUS

Swallows have built nests in Cleopatra's sails. The fortunetellers won't say whether that's a good sign or a bad one, but they don't look happy. Antony is valiant and dejected. His mood changes by fits and starts; his checkered luck vacillates between hope and fear, winning and losing.

ANTONY *enters.*

ANTONY

All is lost! This treacherous Egyptian has betrayed me. My fleet has surrendered to the enemy. You can see them over there throwing their hats up in the air and drinking together like long lost friends. Three-time traitor and whore! It's you who have sold me to this youth, Caesar. Now my war is only with you. Tell the army to flee. Revenge on Cleopatra will be my last act. Order them to escape. Go!

> SCARUS *exits.*

Oh, sun, I will never see another one of your sunrises. Luck and Antony separate here and now. Here we'll shake hands good-bye. Is it all come to this? The brave

That spanieled me at heels, to whom I gave
Their wishes, do discandy, melt their sweets
On blossoming Caesar, and this pine is barked
That overtopped them all. Betrayed I am.
25 Oh, this false soul of Egypt! This grave charm,
Whose eye becked forth my wars and called them home,
Whose bosom was my crownet, my chief end,
Like a right gypsy hath at fast and loose
Beguiled me to the very heart of loss.
30 *(calling out)* What, Eros, Eros!

Enter CLEOPATRA

                                    Ah, thou spell! Avaunt!

CLEOPATRA
Why is my lord enraged against his love?

ANTONY
Vanish, or I shall give thee thy deserving,
And blemish Caesar's triumph. Let him take thee
And hoist thee up to the shouting plebeians!
35 Follow his chariot, like the greatest spot
Of all thy sex. Most monsterlike be shown
For poor'st diminutives, for dolts, and let
Patient Octavia plow thy visage up
With her preparèd nails!

                                    Exit CLEOPATRA
                          'Tis well th'art gone,
40 If it be well to live, but better 'twere
Thou fell'st into my fury, for one death
Might have prevented many.—Eros, ho!—
The shirt of Nessus is upon me. Teach me,
Alcides, thou mine ancestor, thy rage.
45 Let me lodge Lichas on the horns o' th' moon,
And with those hands that grasped the heaviest club
Subdue my worthiest self. The witch shall die.

men who followed me like little dogs, whom I rewarded, have left me to follow Caesar. I've been stripped of everything, betrayed. Oh, that devious Egyptian spirit! Her charms launched my wars and called them back again. Pleasing her was my main goal, and she lured me to total defeat. *(calling out)* Where are you, Eros! Eros!

CLEOPATRA *enters.*

Ah, you sorceress! Be gone!

CLEOPATRA

Why is my lord enraged against his love?

ANTONY

Get out of my sight, or I'll give you what you deserve and spoil Caesar's victory. Let him hoist you up in front of the shouting crowds! Follow his chariot, like the greatest disgrace to your whole gender. Let them exhibit you to the public for meager coins, like a monstrosity. Then let Octavia dig up your face with her nails.

CLEOPATRA *exits.*

If you wish to live, you had better get out of here. But I think it would have been better if you'd let me kill you. One death would have prevented the deaths of many others.—Eros, ho!—I'm wearing the shirt of Nessus. Hercules, my ancestor, teach me how to feel your rage. I'll toss Lichas to the moon and use my mighty hands to kill my better self. The witch shall die.

Hercules was killed by a shirt poisoned with Nessus' blood. Wild with pain, he threw his servant Lichas all the way to the sea.

To the young Roman boy she hath sold me, and I fall
Under this plot. She dies for 't.—Eros, ho!

Exit

She sold me to that young Roman boy and now I'm ruined. She'll die for it.—Eros, ho!

He exits.

ACT 4, SCENE 13

Enter CLEOPATRA, CHARMIAN, IRAS, *and* MARDIAN

CLEOPATRA
Help me, my women! Oh, he's more mad
Than Telamon for his shield. The boar of Thessaly
Was never so embossed.

CHARMIAN
                                        To th' monument!
There lock yourself and send him word you are dead.
5   The soul and body rive not more in parting
Than greatness going off.

CLEOPATRA
                                        To th' monument!—
Mardian, go tell him I have slain myself.
Say that the last I spoke was "Antony,"
And word it, prithee, piteously. Hence, Mardian,
10   And bring me how he takes my death. *(to the others)*
To th' monument!

                                                            Exeunt

ACT 4, SCENE 13

CLEOPATRA, CHARMIAN, IRAS, *and* MARDIAN *enter.*

CLEOPATRA

Help me, ladies! Oh, Antony is more furious than Telamon, who killed himself in a jealous rage. The wild boar of Thessaly, which the goddess Diana sent to punish King Caledon for neglecting her sacrifices, didn't foam at the mouth as much as Antony does now.

CHARMIAN

Go to your tomb! Lock yourself in and send him word that you're dead. When a great person departs, it causes more pain than when the soul leaves the body.

CLEOPATRA

To my tomb! Mardian, go tell him I've killed myself. Say the last word I spoke was "Antony," and please word it pathetically. Go, Mardian, and let me know how he reacts to my death. *(to the others)* To the tomb!

They all exit.

ACT 4, SCENE 14

Enter ANTONY *and* EROS

ANTONY
Eros, thou yet behold'st me?

EROS
                                        Ay, noble lord.

ANTONY
Sometimes we see a cloud that's dragonish,
A vapor sometime like a bear or lion,
A towered citadel, a pendant rock,
5   A forkèd mountain, or blue promontory
With trees upon 't that nod unto the world
And mock our eyes with air. Thou hast seen these signs.
They are black vesper's pageants.

EROS
                                        Ay, my lord.

ANTONY
That which is now a horse, even with a thought
10   The rack dislimns and makes it indistinct
As water is in water.

EROS
                              It does, my lord.

ANTONY
My good knave Eros, now thy captain is
Even such a body. Here I am Antony,
Yet cannot hold this visible shape, my knave.
15   I made these wars for Egypt, and the Queen,
Whose heart I thought I had, for she had mine—
Which whilst it was mine had annexed unto 't
A million more, now lost—she, Eros, has
Packed cards with Caesar and false-played my glory
20   Unto an enemy's triumph.
Nay, weep not, gentle Eros. There is left us
Ourselves to end ourselves.

ACT 4, SCENE 14

ANTONY *and* EROS *enter.*

ANTONY

Eros, can you still see me?

EROS

Yes, noble lord.

ANTONY

Sometimes we see a cloud that looks like a dragon. Sometimes there's a cloud like a bear or a lion, a castle, a floating rock, a craggy mountain. Or it might look like a blue cliff with trees on it that bow to the ground. These things fool our eyes by seeming solid, when they are actually only air. You've seen these illusions. They're spectacles that appear at sunset.

EROS

Yes, my lord.

ANTONY

What looks like a horse is quick as thought disfigured by the wind, made as difficult to distinguish as water poured into water.

EROS

That's true, my lord.

ANTONY

Eros, my young friend, your captain is now just like that cloud. Here and now I seem like Antony, but I can't keep myself in this form, my boy. I went to war to save Cleopatra, whose love I thought I had, since she had mine—and mine carried with it a million others, those of my soldiers, now lost. The Queen conspired with Caesar to undermine my success and assure his victory. No, don't cry, kind Eros. We still have the option of killing ourselves.

Enter MARDIAN

                                        Oh, thy vile lady!
She has robbed me of my sword.

MARDIAN
                                        No, Antony,
My mistress loved thee, and her fortunes mingled
With thine entirely.

ANTONY
                                        Hence, saucy eunuch! Peace!
She hath betrayed me and shall die the death.

MARDIAN
Death of one person can be paid but once,
And that she has discharged. What thou wouldst do
Is done unto thy hand. The last she spake
Was "Antony, most noble Antony!"
Then in the midst a tearing groan did break
The name of Antony. It was divided
Between her heart and lips. She rendered life,
Thy name so buried in her.

ANTONY
                                        Dead, then?

MARDIAN
                                                Dead.

ANTONY
Unarm, Eros. The long day's task is done,
And we must sleep. *(to* MARDIAN*)* That thou depart'st hence
        safe
Does pay thy labor richly. Go.

                                        Exit MARDIAN
                                Off, pluck off!
The sevenfold shield of Ajax cannot keep
The battery from my heart. O, cleave, my sides!
Heart, once be stronger than thy continent.
Crack thy frail case!—Apace, Eros, apace.

MARDIAN *enters.*

Oh, your contemptible lady! She has disarmed me.

MARDIAN

No, Antony. My mistress loved you, and her destiny was completely joined with yours.

ANTONY

Get out, insolent eunuch! Silence! She has betrayed me and shall die.

MARDIAN

A person can only pay with their life once, and she has paid in full. What you wanted is yours. Her last words were "Antony! Most noble Antony!" Then, as she was speaking your name, a strangled groan split her words. "Antony" was divided between her heart and lips. She gave up her life with your name still within her.

ANTONY

Is she dead, then?

MARDIAN

Dead.

ANTONY

Remove your armor, Eros. The long day's work is over, and it is time to sleep. *(to* MARDIAN*)* Permission to leave unharmed is abundant payment for your news. Go!

MARDIAN *exits.*

Off! Take off my armor. Not even Ajax's famous shield, made of seven layers of oxhide and covered in bronze, could protect my heart from this attack. Oh, chest, obey me! Heart, for once be stronger than all the rest of the body combined. Break out of my ribcage! Faster, Eros, faster. I won't be a soldier anymore.

No more a soldier. Bruisèd pieces, go.
You have been nobly borne. *(to* EROS*)* From me awhile.

Exit EROS

I will o'ertake thee, Cleopatra, and
45   Weep for my pardon. So it must be, for now
All length is torture. Since the torch is out,
Lie down and stray no farther. Now all labor
Mars what it does. Yea, very force entangles
Itself with strength. Seal then, and all is done.—
50   Eros!—I come, my Queen.—Eros!—Stay for me.
Where souls do couch on flowers, we'll hand in hand,
And with our sprightly port make the ghosts gaze.
Dido and her Aeneas shall want troops,
And all the haunt be ours.—Come, Eros, Eros!

Enter EROS

EROS
55   . What would my lord?

ANTONY
Since Cleopatra died
I have lived in such dishonor that the gods
Detest my baseness. I, that with my sword
Quartered the world, and o'er green Neptune's back
With ships made cities, condemn myself to lack
60   The courage of a woman—less noble mind
Than she which by her death our Caesar tells
"I am conqueror of myself." Thou art sworn, Eros,
That when the exigent should come which now
Is come indeed, when I should see behind me
65   Th' inevitable prosecution of
Disgrace and horror, that on my command,
Thou then wouldst kill me. Do 't. The time is come.
Thou strik'st not me, 'tis Caesar thou defeat'st.
Put color in thy cheek.

Battered armor, be off. You were worn with honor. *(to*
EROS*)* Leave me awhile.

EROS exits.

I will catch up with you, Cleopatra, and weep for your
forgiveness. It's the only way left, because now any
extension of my life would be torture. Since the light
of my life has gone out, I'll stop here. Now any effort
ruins what it attempts. Yes, even power gets in its own
way. End it, then, and everything is over.—Eros!—
I'm coming, my Queen!—Eros!—Wait for me. In the
place where souls recline on beds of flowers we'll walk
hand in hand and amaze the other ghosts with our
spirited demeanor. Those famous lovers, Dido and
Aeneas, will lose their admirers, and the whole place
will be devoted to us.—Come, Eros. Eros!

EROS *enters.*

EROS

What can I do for my lord?

ANTONY

Since Cleopatra died, I have lived in such dishonor
that the gods despise my disgrace. Though I have
made conquests throughout the four corners of the
world and sailed with fleets so large they looked like
floating cities, I don't have as much courage as a
woman. I have less nobility than the lady who, by killing herself, says to Caesar, "Only Cleopatra can defeat
Cleopatra." You promised me, Eros, that should the
ultimate moment arrive—which it has—when dishonor and disgust are inevitable, that upon my command, you would kill me. Do it. This is that time. You
won't be striking me down, but defeating Caesar. Call
up your courage.

EROS

                            The gods withhold me!
70   Shall I do that which all the Parthian darts,
        Though enemy, lost aim and could not?

ANTONY

                                    Eros,
        Wouldst thou be windowed in great Rome and see
        Thy master thus with pleached arms, bending down
        His corrigible neck, his face subdued
75   To penetrative shame, whilst the wheeled seat
        Of fortunate Caesar, drawn before him, branded
        His baseness that ensued?

EROS

                            I would not see 't.

ANTONY

        Come, then, for with a wound I must be cured.
        Draw that thy honest sword, which thou hast worn
80   Most useful for thy country.

EROS

                            O sir, pardon me!

ANTONY

        When I did make thee free, swor'st thou not then
        To do this when I bade thee? Do it at once,
        Or thy precedent services are all
        But accidents unpurposed. Draw and come.

EROS
85   Turn from me then that noble countenance
        Wherein the worship of the whole world lies.

ANTONY
        Lo thee!

        He turns away

EROS
        My sword is drawn.

EROS

The gods forbid! Can I do what all the Parthian arrows, though shot by enemies, could not?

ANTONY

Eros, would you like to look through a window in Rome and watch your master marching in Caesar's victory parade, his arms crossed and tied, his head bowed in submission, his face red from shame, while the chariot of triumphant Caesar precedes him, putting the final stamp to his humiliation?

EROS

I would not.

ANTONY

Then come on. I must be restored to health by an injury. Draw your trustworthy sword, which you have used in such service to your country.

EROS

Oh, sir, pardon me!

ANTONY

When I freed you from slavery, didn't you swear to do this when I asked you? Do it immediately, or all your previous services to me were accidental, without purpose. Take out your sword and come on.

EROS

Then turn your noble face away from me, that face that the whole world adores.

ANTONY

Look!

He turns away.

EROS

I have drawn my sword.

ANTONY
                                        Then let it do at once
   The thing why thou hast drawn it.

EROS
                                        My dear master,
90   My captain, and my emperor, let me say,
   Before I strike this bloody stroke, farewell.

ANTONY
   'Tis said, man, and farewell.

EROS
   Farewell, great chief. Shall I strike now?

ANTONY
                                        Now, Eros.

EROS
   Why, there then!

   Stabs himself

                        Thus I do escape the sorrow
95   Of Antony's death.

   He dies

ANTONY
                        Thrice nobler than myself,
   Thou teachest me, O valiant Eros, what
   I should and thou couldst not. My Queen and Eros
   Have by their brave instruction got upon me
   A nobleness in record. But I will be
100   A bridegroom in my death, and run into 't
   As to a lover's bed. Come then, and Eros,
   Thy master dies thy scholar. To do thus
   I learned of thee.

   He falls on his sword

ANTONY

Now let it carry out its purpose immediately.

EROS

My dear master, my captain, my sovereign, let me say before I strike this fatal blow: farewell.

ANTONY

You've said it, friend, and farewell to you.

EROS

Good-bye, great commander. Should I do it now?

ANTONY

Now, Eros.

EROS

Well, then, there!

He stabs himself.

With this I avoid the grief of Antony's death.

He dies.

ANTONY

Brave Eros, three times more honorable than I am! You teach me what I should do but could not. My Queen and Eros have by their brave examples beaten me to the history books. But I will embrace death as a bridegroom does his bride, and rush to it as to a lover's bed. Come then. Eros, your master dies your student. I learned to do this from you.

He falls on his sword.

How! Not dead? Not dead?
The guard, ho! Oh, dispatch me!

Enter DERCETUS *and others of a* GUARD

FIRST GUARD
105   What's the noise?

ANTONY
I have done my work ill, friends. Oh, make an end
Of what I have begun!

SECOND GUARD
                 The star is fall'n.

FIRST GUARD
And time is at his period.

ALL
                Alas, and woe!

ANTONY
Let him that loves me strike me dead.

FIRST GUARD
110   Not I.

SECOND GUARD
Nor I.

THIRD GUARD
Nor anyone.

Exeunt GUARD

DERCETUS
Thy death and fortunes bid thy followers fly.

He takes up ANTONY's *sword*

This sword but shown to Caesar, with this tidings,
115   Shall enter me with him.

Enter DIOMEDES

What! I'm not dead? Not dead?—Guard, here! Oh,
kill me!

DERCETUS enters with three GUARDS.

FIRST GUARD

What's the trouble?

ANTONY

I've botched the job, friends. Oh, finish what I've
begun.

SECOND GUARD

Our guiding light is out.

FIRST GUARD

And time itself is ended.

ALL

Sadness and despair!

ANTONY

Whoever's a real friend should strike me dead.

FIRST GUARD

Not me.

SECOND GUARD

Me neither.

THIRD GUARD

None of us.

The GUARDS exit.

DERCETAS

Your death and destiny advise your followers to escape.

He takes up ANTONY's sword

I only need to show your sword to Caesar and tell him
about your death to get into his good favor.

DIOMEDES enters.

DIOMEDES
Where's Antony?

DERCETUS
There, Diomed, there.

DIOMEDES
Lives he? Wilt thou not answer, man?

Exit DERCETUS

ANTONY
Art thou there, Diomed? Draw thy sword and give me
120   Sufficing strokes for death.

DIOMEDES
                                        Most absolute lord,
My mistress Cleopatra sent me to thee.

ANTONY
When did she send thee?

DIOMEDES
                                        Now, my lord.

ANTONY
                                                Where is she?

DIOMEDES
Locked in her monument. She had a prophesying fear
Of what hath come to pass. For when she saw—
125   Which never shall be found—you did suspect
She had disposed with Caesar, and that your rage
Would not be purged, she sent you word she was dead.
But fearing since how it might work, hath sent
Me to proclaim the truth, and I am come,
130   I dread, too late.

ANTONY
Too late, good Diomed. Call my guard, I prithee.

DIOMEDES
What ho, the Emperor's guard! The guard, what ho!
Come, your lord calls!

Enter four or five of the GUARD *of Antony*

DIOMEDES

Where's Antony?

DERCETAS

There, Diomedes, there.

DIOMEDES

Is he still alive? Why don't you answer me, man?

DERCETAS exits.

ANTONY

Is that you, Diomedes? Draw your sword and give me enough blows to kill me.

DIOMEDES

Most powerful lord, my mistress Cleopatra sent me to you.

ANTONY

When did she send you?

DIOMEDES

Just now, my lord.

ANTONY

Where is she?

DIOMEDES

Locked in her tomb. She had a premonition of what has actually happened. She saw that you suspected her of negotiating a treaty with Caesar—which never will be true. Afraid that your anger would not subside, she sent you word she was dead. But later, fearing how that news might affect you, she sent me to tell you the truth. I'm afraid I've come too late.

ANTONY

Too late, good Diomedes. Call my guard, please.

DIOMEDES

Hey out there! Emperor's guards! Guards, hey! Come! Your lord calls for you!

Four or five of Antony's GUARDS *enter.*

ANTONY
> Bear me, good friends, where Cleopatra bides.
> 135 'Tis the last service that I shall command you.

FIRST GUARD
> Woe, woe are we, sir, you may not live to wear
> All your true followers out.

ALL
>   Most heavy day!

ANTONY
> Nay, good my fellows, do not please sharp fate
> To grace it with your sorrows. Bid that welcome
> 140 Which comes to punish us, and we punish it,
> Seeming to bear it lightly. Take me up.
> I have led you oft; carry me now, good friends,
> And have my thanks for all.
>   *Exeunt, bearing* ANTONY *and the body of* EROS

ANTONY

Carry me, good friends, to where Cleopatra is. It's the last command I shall ever give you.

FIRST GUARD

We're very sorry, sir, that you may not live to wear us out with your commands.

ALL

It's a very sad day.

ANTONY

No, my friends, don't please fate by giving it your sorrow as well. If we welcome our punishment, we punish it right back by seeming to take it lightly. Pick me up. I have often led you, now you must carry me, my good friends—and take my thanks for everything.

They exit, carrying ANTONY *and* EROS' *body.*

ACT 4, SCENE 15

Enter CLEOPATRA *and her maids aloft, with* CHARMIAN
and IRAS

CLEOPATRA
O Charmian, I will never go from hence.

CHARMIAN
Be comforted, dear madam.

CLEOPATRA
                              No, I will not.
All strange and terrible events are welcome,
But comforts we despise. Our size of sorrow,
Proportioned to our cause, must be as great
As that which makes it.

Enter below DIOMEDES

                              How now? Is he dead?

DIOMEDES
His death's upon him, but not dead.
Look out o' th' other side your monument.
His guard have brought him thither.

Enter below ANTONY, *and the guard bearing him*

CLEOPATRA
                              O sun,
Burn the great sphere thou mov'st in. Darkling stand
The varying shore o' th' world! O Antony,
Antony, Antony! Help, Charmian, help, Iras, help!
Help, friends below! Let's draw him hither.

ANTONY
                              Peace!
Not Caesar's valor hath o'erthrown Antony,
But Antony's hath triumphed on itself.

ACT 4, SCENE 15

CLEOPATRA, CHARMIAN, *and* IRAS *enter with Cleopatra's maids in the upper gallery.*

CLEOPATRA

Oh, Charmian, I will never leave this tomb!

CHARMIAN

Be calm, dear lady.

CLEOPATRA

No, I won't. Strange and terrible events are all welcome, but I despise comforts. The size of my sorrow must be as great as its source.

DIOMEDES *enters below.*

What's the news! Is he dead?

DIOMEDES

He is close to death, but not dead yet. Look out the other window; his guard has brought him here.

Guards enter, carrying ANTONY.

CLEOPATRA

Oh, sun, burn up the orbit in which you move, so that the world may be dark forever! Oh, Antony, Antony, Antony! Help, Charmian, help, Iras, help! Help, friends below; lift him up here.

ANTONY

Be calm! It was not Caesar's bravery that conquered Antony but Antony's that has triumphed over himself.

CLEOPATRA

    So it should be, that none but Antony

    Should conquer Antony, but woe 'tis so!

ANTONY

    I am dying, Egypt, dying. Only

    I here importune death awhile, until

20   Of many thousand kisses the poor last

    I lay upon thy lips.

CLEOPATRA

                I dare not, dear,

    Dear my lord, pardon, I dare not,

    Lest I be taken. Not th' imperious show

    Of the full-fortuned Caesar ever shall

25   Be brooched with me. If knife, drugs, serpents, have

    Edge, sting, or operation, I am safe.

    Your wife Octavia, with her modest eyes

    And still conclusion, shall acquire no honor

    Demuring upon me. But come, come, Antony—

30   Help me, my women—We must draw thee up.

    Assist, good friends.

They begin lifting him

ANTONY

               Oh, quick, or I am gone.

CLEOPATRA

    Here's sport indeed! How heavy weighs my lord!

    Our strength is all gone into heaviness,

    That makes the weight. Had I great Juno's power,

35   The strong-winged Mercury should fetch thee up

    And set thee by Jove's side. Yet come a little.

    Wishers were ever fools. Oh, come, come, come!

They heave **ANTONY** *aloft to* **CLEOPATRA**

CLEOPATRA

> That's the way it should be—only Antony should conquer Antony. But how terrible that it has happened!

ANTONY

> I am dying, Cleopatra, dying. I just beg death to wait awhile, until I place the last of our many thousands of kisses on your lips.

CLEOPATRA

> I don't dare come down—forgive me, my lord—I don't dare, for fear of capture. I will never be exhibited as lucky Caesar's prize. If knives, poison, or snakes have edge, effect, or venom, I am safe from that fate. Your wife Octavia, with her self-effacing eyes and self-righteous assumptions, won't get any praise from patronizing me. But come. Come up here, Antony—help me, ladies—we must carry you up. Help us, good friends.

They lift him.

ANTONY

> Oh, quick, before I'm gone.

CLEOPATRA

> Such exercise! My lord is so heavy! Our strength has all turned into sadness. That's what makes the weight. If I had the goddess Juno's power, I would make the strong-winged messenger, Mercury, pick you up and seat you beside Jove. Up just a little more—wishes are always foolish—oh, come on, come on, come on!

They lift **ANTONY** *up to* **CLEOPATRA**.

And welcome, welcome! Die when thou hast lived.
Quicken with kissing. Had my lips that power,
40   Thus would I wear them out.

She kisses him

ALL
A heavy sight!
ANTONY
I am dying, Egypt, dying.
Give me some wine and let me speak a little.
CLEOPATRA
No, let me speak, and let me rail so high
45   That the false huswife Fortune break her wheel,
Provoked by my offense.

ANTONY
                              One word, sweet Queen:
Of Caesar seek your honor, with your safety—Oh!
CLEOPATRA
They do not go together.
ANTONY
                              Gentle, hear me.
None about Caesar trust but Proculeius.
CLEOPATRA
50   My resolution and my hands I'll trust,
None about Caesar.
ANTONY
The miserable change now at my end
Lament nor sorrow at, but please your thoughts
In feeding them with those my former fortunes,
55   Wherein I lived the greatest prince o' th' world,
The noblest, and do now not basely die,
Not cowardly put off my helmet to
My countryman—a Roman by a Roman

And welcome, welcome! Die where you have lived, in my arms. Let me revive you with my kisses. If my lips had the power to give life, I would wear them out like this.

She kisses him.

ALL

What a sad sight!

ANTONY

I am dying, Cleopatra, dying. Give me some wine and let me say a few words.

CLEOPATRA

Fortune was often depicted as a woman with a wheel, which controlled human beings' fates.

No, let me talk, and let me scold to the heavens, so that Fortune, that deceitful hussy, will become so upset that she breaks her wheel.

ANTONY

One thing, dear Queen: request honor, as well as safety, from Caesar. Oh!

CLEOPATRA

Honor and safety do not go together.

ANTONY

Dear, listen to me: don't trust any of Caesar's men besides Proculeius.

CLEOPATRA

I'll trust my determination and my hands, but none of Caesar's men.

ANTONY

Don't mourn over this unhappy reversal of fortune at the end of my life. Remember my earlier lot, when I lived as the greatest, most noble prince in the world. I'm not dying shamefully, doffing my helmet to my countryman like a coward, but as a Roman, honorably conquered by another Roman.

Valiantly vanquished. Now my spirit is going.
60   I can no more.

CLEOPATRA

                    Noblest of men, woo't die?
Hast thou no care of me? Shall I abide
In this dull world, which in thy absence is
No better than a sty? O see, my women,
The crown o' th' earth doth melt. My lord!

ANTONY *dies*

65   Oh, withered is the garland of the war.
The soldier's pole is fall'n! Young boys and girls
Are level now with men. The odds is gone,
And there is nothing left remarkable
Beneath the visiting moon.

CHARMIAN

                    Oh, quietness, lady!

CLEOPATRA *swoons*

IRAS
70   She's dead too, our sovereign.

CHARMIAN
Lady!

IRAS
Madam!

CHARMIAN
O madam, madam, madam!

IRAS
Royal Egypt, Empress!

CLEOPATRA *stirs*

CHARMIAN
75   Peace, peace, Iras.

Now I feel my soul leaving. I can't speak any more.

CLEOPATRA

Most noble man, will you die? Don't you care about me? Shall I stay in this dreary world, which is no better than a pigsty without you? Oh, look, ladies. The best of the world disappears. My lord!

ANTONY *dies.*

Oh, the glory of war has faded. The flags have fallen. Young boys and girls are equal to men. There is nothing distinctive, nothing remarkable left in the world.

CHARMIAN

Oh, stay calm, lady!

CLEOPATRA *faints.*

IRAS

Our Queen is dead too.

CHARMIAN

Lady!

IRAS

Madam!

CHARMIAN

Oh, madam, madam, madam!

IRAS

Royal Egypt, Empress!

CLEOPATRA *wakes up.*

CHARMIAN

Quiet, quiet, Iras.

CLEOPATRA
No more but e'en a woman, and commanded
By such poor passion as the maid that milks
And does the meanest chares. It were for me
To throw my scepter at the injurious gods,
80   To tell them that this world did equal theirs
Till they had stolen our jewel. All's but naught.
Patience is sottish, and impatience does
Become a dog that's mad. Then is it sin
To rush into the secret house of death
85   Ere death dare come to us? How do you, women?
What, what, good cheer! Why, how now, Charmian?
My noble girls! Ah, women, women! Look,
Our lamp is spent, it's out. Good sirs, take heart.
We'll bury him, and then, what's brave, what's noble,
90   Let's do 't after the high Roman fashion
And make death proud to take us. Come, away.
This case of that huge spirit now is cold.
Ah, women, women! Come. We have no friend
But resolution, and the briefest end.
                    Exeunt, those above bearing off **ANTONY**'s *body*

CLEOPATRA

Now I am no more than a woman, ruled by the same lowly passion as the maid who milks and does the humblest chores. I might now hurl my scepter at the destructive gods and tell them that this earthly world was as good as their heavenly one, until they stole away its jewel, Antony. Now all is for nothing. Patience is foolish. Impatience suits a mad dog. So why should it be a sin to rush toward death, to seek it out in its hiding place before it dares to come to find me? How are you, my ladies? Tell me! Cheer up! How are you, Charmian? My gallant girls! Ah, ladies, look: the light of our lives has gone out. Good noble ladies, be brave. We'll bury him, and then we'll commit acts as brave and fine as any Romans, and make death proud to take us. Come on, you can go. The container of that great soul is now cold. Ah, ladies, ladies! Let's go. We have no friends but determination and the quickest death.

They exit, carrying ANTONY's *body.*

ACT FIVE

SCENE 1

Enter CAESAR, *with* AGRIPPA, DOLABELLA, MAECENAS,
GALLUS, *and* PROCULEIUS, *and his council of war*

CAESAR
> Go to him, Dolabella, bid him yield.
> Being so frustrate, tell him, he mocks
> The pauses that he makes.

DOLABELLA
>   Caesar, I shall.

>   *Exit*

Enter DERCETUS, *with the sword of* ANTONY

CAESAR
> Wherefore is that? And what art thou that dar'st
> Appear thus to us?

DERCETUS
>   I am called Dercetus.
> Mark Antony I served, who best was worthy
> Best to be served. Whilst he stood up and spoke,
> He was my master, and I wore my life
> To spend upon his haters. If thou please
> To take me to thee, as I was to him
> I'll be to Caesar. If thou pleasest not,
> I yield thee up my life.

CAESAR
>   What is 't thou say'st?

DERCETUS
> I say, O Caesar, Antony is dead.

CAESAR
> The breaking of so great a thing should make
> A greater crack. The round world

ACT FIVE
SCENE 1

CAESAR *enters with his war council:* AGRIPPA,
DOLABELLA, MAECENAS, GALLUS, *and* PROCULEIUS.

CAESAR

Dolabella, go see Antony. Tell him to surrender. His position is hopeless. This delay makes him look ridiculous.

DOLABELLA

Right away, Caesar.

DOLABELLA exits.

DECRETUS *enters carrying* ANTONY'*s sword.*

CAESAR

What are you doing with a sword? Who do you think you are coming in here armed?

DECRETUS

My name is Decretus. I served Mark Antony, who was the commander most worthy of my services. While he was alive, I lived only to serve him and oppose his enemies. If you accept my service, I'll serve you the same way. If not, you can kill me.

CAESAR

What are you saying?

DECRETUS

Caesar, I'm telling you that Antony is dead.

CAESAR

When such a great man dies there should be a thunderclap. The fractured world, in its confusion, should

Should have shook lions into civil streets
And citizens to their dens. The death of Antony
Is not a single doom. In the name lay
A moiety of the world.

DERCETUS

He is dead, Caesar,
20   Not by a public minister of justice,
Nor by a hirèd knife, but that self hand
Which writ his honor in the acts it did
Hath, with the courage which the heart did lend it,
Splitted the heart. This is his sword.
25   I robbed his wound of it. Behold it stained
With his most noble blood.

CAESAR

Look you, sad friends,
The gods rebuke me, but it is tidings
To wash the eyes of kings.

AGRIPPA

And strange it is
That nature must compel us to lament
30   Our most persisted deeds.

MAECENAS

His taints and honors
Waged equal with him.

AGRIPPA

A rarer spirit never
Did steer humanity, but you gods will give us
Some faults to make us men. Caesar is touched.

MAECENAS

When such a spacious mirror's set before him,
35   He needs must see himself.

CAESAR

O Antony,
I have followed thee to this, but we do launch
Diseases in our bodies. I must perforce
Have shown to thee such a declining day,

send lions into the city streets and humans into the wilderness to live in lions' dens. This isn't the death of one man. It's the death of half the world.

DECRETUS

He's dead, Caesar. Not by public execution or an assassin's knife. He killed himself with the same hand that performed such brave acts. With the courage his heart lent his hand, his hand in turn split his heart. This is his sword. I pulled it from his wound. Look— his noble blood is still on it.

CAESAR

Listen, sad friends, though the gods may rebuke me, this news would make kings cry.

AGRIPPA

It's strange that human nature makes us grieve for the very thing we've been trying to achieve.

MAECENAS

His faults were equally matched by his virtues.

AGRIPPA

There was never a ruler as excellent as he. But gods, you give us faults so we'll be human. Caesar is upset.

MAECENAS

It's impossible for him not to see himself in Antony.

CAESAR

Oh, Antony. I drove you to this. But we have to get rid of a disease if it threatens our body. Either I had to ruin you, or you would have ruined me.

Or look on thine. We could not stall together
40   In the whole world. But yet let me lament
With tears as sovereign as the blood of hearts
That thou, my brother, my competitor
In top of all design, my mate in empire,
Friend and companion in the front of war,
45   The arm of mine own body, and the heart
Where mine his thoughts did kindle—that our stars,
Unreconcilable, should divide
Our equalness to this. Hear me, good friends—

Enter an EGYPTIAN

But I will tell you at some meeter season.
50   The business of this man looks out of him.
We'll hear him what he says. *(to* EGYPTIAN*)* Whence are
you?

EGYPTIAN
A poor Egyptian yet, the Queen my mistress,
Confined in all she has, her monument,
Of thy intents desires instruction,
55   That she preparedly may frame herself
To th' way she's forced to.

CAESAR
                              Bid her have good heart.
She soon shall know of us, by some of ours,
How honorable and how kindly we
Determine for her, for Caesar cannot live
60   To be ungentle.

EGYPTIAN
                    So the gods preserve thee!

                                          Exit

CAESAR
Come hither, Proculeius. Go and say
We purpose her no shame. Give her what comforts
The quality of her passion shall require,

There wasn't enough room in the world for both of us. Even so, let me mourn, with tears that heal like a bloodletting, that you—my brother, my greatest competitor, my partner in rule, my friend and companion on the battlefield, the very arm of my body, and the heart in which mine own heart's thoughts lived—that our fates could not be reconciled, which caused us to divide ourselves from one another.

Let me tell you, friends—

An EGYPTIAN *enters.*

I'll tell you at a better time. This man looks like his business is urgent. Let's hear what he has to say. *(to* EGYPTIAN*)* Who are you?

EGYPTIAN

A poor Egyptian, but my mistress, the Queen, sent me to find out what your intentions are concerning her. She's locked up in her tomb and wants to prepare herself for her fate.

CAESAR

Tell her to put her mind at rest. She'll find out soon enough by one of our messengers how respectfully and kindly we plan to treat her. I cannot be taught how to be cruel.

EGYPTIAN

May the gods bless you.

He exits.

CAESAR

Come here, Proculeius. Tell her we mean her no disrespect. Give her whatever assurances you feel she needs to keep her from killing herself. I need her alive,

Lest, in her greatness, by some mortal stroke
65 She do defeat us, for her life in Rome
Would be eternal in our triumph. Go,
And with your speediest bring us what she says
And how you find of her.

PROCULEIUS
                        Caesar, I shall.

Exit PROCULEIUS

CAESAR
Gallus, go you along.

Exit GALLUS

                        Where's Dolabella,
70 To second Proculeius?

ALL
                        Dolabella!

CAESAR
Let him alone, for I remember now
How he's employed. He shall in time be ready.
Go with me to my tent, where you shall see
How hardly I was drawn into this war,
75 How calm and gentle I proceeded still
In all my writings. Go with me and see
What I can show in this.

Exeunt

so that I can exhibit her in my triumphal procession and gain eternal fame. Go, and hurry back to bring us her reply and news of her state of mind.

PROCULEIUS

I will, Caesar.

PROCULEIUS exits.

CAESAR

Gallus, you go with him.

GALLUS exits.

Where's Dolabella? He's supposed to support Proculeius.

ALL

Dolabella!

CAESAR

Never mind. I remember he's already occupied. He'll be done in time. Come with me. In my tent I'll show you how unwillingly I was drawn into this war. You'll see how calm and gentle my letters to Antony always were. Come and see the proof.

They exit.

ACT 5, SCENE 2

Enter CLEOPATRA, CHARMIAN, *and* IRAS

CLEOPATRA
My desolation does begin to make
A better life. 'Tis paltry to be Caesar.
Not being Fortune, he's but Fortune's knave,
A minister of her will. And it is great
5   To do that thing that ends all other deeds,
Which shackles accidents and bolts up change,
Which sleeps and never palates more the dung,
The beggar's nurse, and Caesar's.

Enter PROCULEIUS

PROCULEIUS
Caesar sends greeting to the Queen of Egypt,
10   And bids thee study on what fair demands
Thou mean'st to have him grant thee.

CLEOPATRA
                                        What's thy name?

PROCULEIUS
My name is Proculeius.

CLEOPATRA
                              Antony
Did tell me of you, bade me trust you, but
I do not greatly care to be deceived,
15   That have no use for trusting. If your master
Would have a queen his beggar, you must tell him,
That majesty, to keep decorum, must
No less beg than a kingdom. If he please
To give me conquered Egypt for my son,
20   He gives me so much of mine own as I
Will kneel to him with thanks.

ACT 5, SCENE 2

CLEOPATRA, CHARMIAN, *and* IRAS *enter.*

Being alone has helped me better understand my life. It's pathetic to be Caesar. He can't be Fortune; he's only Fortune's errand boy. It would be a great deed to commit suicide—that act which ends all other things, which makes all accidents and changes stop. Which causes you to sleep, and takes you away from earthly concerns.

PROCULEIUS *enters.*

PROCULEIUS
Caesar greets the Queen of Egypt and asks that you consider what you will ask from him.

CLEOPATRA
What's your name?

PROCULEIUS
My name is Proculeius.

CLEOPATRA
Antony told me about you. He said you were a man I could trust. But I don't worry about being deceived because I don't need to trust. If your master wants a queen to beg from him, you should tell him that a queen will beg for no less than a kingdom.

If he will grant me conquered Egypt, so that I may give it to my son, I will kneel to him with thanks.

PROCULEIUS
                                    Be of good cheer.
You're fall'n into a princely hand. Fear nothing.
Make your full reference freely to my lord,
Who is so full of grace that it flows over
On all that need. Let me report to him
Your sweet dependency, and you shall find
A conqueror that will pray in aid for kindness
Where he for grace is kneeled to.

CLEOPATRA
                                    Pray you, tell him
I am his fortune's vassal, and I send him
The greatness he has got. I hourly learn
A doctrine of obedience, and would gladly
Look him i' th' face.

PROCULEIUS
                        This I'll report, dear lady.
Have comfort, for I know your plight is pitied
Of him that caused it.

GALLUS and Roman soldiers enter from behind and take
CLEOPATRA prisoner

GALLUS
You see how easily she may be surprised.
(to the soldiers) Guard her till Caesar come.

IRAS
                                    Royal Queen!

CHARMIAN
O Cleopatra! Thou art taken, Queen.

CLEOPATRA draws a dagger

CLEOPATRA
Quick, quick, good hands.

25

30

35

PROCULEIUS

> Be content. You're in the charge of an honorable man. Don't be afraid. You can ask for anything from my lord. His generosity flows to anyone in need. If I can tell him that you have submitted to him sweetly, he'll request your assistance in finding ways in which he can support you.

CLEOPATRA

> Please tell him I have surrendered to his fortune. I give up to him the glory he has won. I'm learning every hour how to be subservient. I'd be happy to meet with him in person.

PROCULEIUS

> I'll tell him all of this, dear lady. Be at ease. I know he's sorry for your situation, especially since he caused it.

> GALLUS *enters with soldiers. They seize* CLEOPATRA.

GALLUS

> *(to* PROCULEIUS*)* See how easy it was to capture her? *(to soldiers)* Guard her until Caesar arrives.

IRAS

> Your majesty!

CHARMIAN

> Oh, Cleopatra! You've been betrayed, my Queen!

> CLEOPATRA *pulls out a knife.*

CLEOPATRA

> Quick, quick good hands!

> PROCULEIUS *seizes the dagger*

PROCULEIUS
                              Hold, worthy lady, hold!
Do not yourself such wrong, who are in this
Relieved but not betrayed.

CLEOPATRA
                              What, of death too,
That rids our dogs of languish?

PROCULEIUS
                                    Cleopatra,
Do not abuse my master's bounty by
Th' undoing of yourself. Let the world see
His nobleness well acted, which your death
Will never let come forth.

CLEOPATRA
                              Where art thou, Death?
Come hither, come! Come, come and take a queen
Worth many babes and beggars!

PROCULEIUS
                              Oh, temperance, lady!

CLEOPATRA
Sir, I will eat no meat, I'll not drink, sir.
If idle talk will once be necessary,
I'll not sleep neither. This mortal house I'll ruin,
Do Caesar what he can. Know, sir, that I
Will not wait pinioned at your master's court,
Nor once be chastised with the sober eye
Of dull Octavia. Shall they hoist me up
And show me to the shouting varletry
Of censuring Rome? Rather a ditch in Egypt
Be gentle grave unto me. Rather on Nilus' mud
Lay me stark naked and let the waterflies
Blow me into abhorring. Rather make
My country's high pyramides my gibbet
And hang me up in chains!

She tries to stab herself, but PROCULEIUS *seizes the dagger.*

PROCULEIUS

Stop, brave lady, stop! Don't do such a shameful thing to yourself. We've rescued you from yourself. We have not betrayed you.

CLEOPATRA

What, am I being denied death, as well? The thing which even dogs are given, to rid them of their suffering?

PROCULEIUS

Don't insult my master's generosity by killing yourself. The world will see how noble he is by the way he treats you. Your death would prevent that.

CLEOPATRA

Where are you, Death? Come here. Come, and you can have a queen. One queen is worth more than a whole number of babies and beggars, your cheapest conquests.

PROCULEIUS

Oh, control yourself, lady!

CLEOPATRA

Sir, I won't eat. I won't drink. And don't expect me to talk. I won't sleep either. I'll destroy my body. Let Caesar do whatever he wants. You'd better understand that I won't wait till I'm chained up in your master's court, and I won't let myself be scolded even once by dull Octavia. Shall I let them exhibit me to the shouting mobs of Rome?

I'd rather die in a ditch in Egypt, and make it my gentle grave. I'd rather lie in the Nile mud with flies laying their eggs in me, making me disgusting. I'd rather be hung in chains from one of our pyramids!

PROCULEIUS
                                        You do extend
These thoughts of horror further than you shall
Find cause in Caesar.

Enter DOLABELLA

DOLABELLA
                                        Proculeius,
What thou hast done thy master Caesar knows,
65   And he hath sent for thee. For the Queen,
I'll take her to my guard.

PROCULEIUS
                                    So, Dolabella,
It shall content me best. Be gentle to her.
(to CLEOPATRA*)* To Caesar I will speak what you shall please,
If you'll employ me to him.

CLEOPATRA
                                    Say I would die.
                                        Exit PROCULEIUS

DOLABELLA
70   Most noble Empress, you have heard of me?

CLEOPATRA
I cannot tell.

DOLABELLA
Assuredly you know me.

CLEOPATRA
No matter, sir, what I have heard or known.
You laugh when boys or women tell their dreams.
75   Is 't not your trick?

DOLABELLA
                                    I understand not, madam.

CLEOPATRA
I dreamt there was an emperor Antony.
Oh, such another sleep, that I might see
But such another man!

PROCULEIUS

> You're letting yourself get carried away with these horrible thoughts. You'll see that Caesar is giving you no reason to do so.

DOLABELLA enters.

DOLABELLA

> Proculeius, Caesar has heard about what you've done here and has sent for you. I'll take the Queen into my custody.

PROCULEIUS

> So be it, Dolabella. Caesar's thanks are my greatest reward. Be kind to her. *(to* CLEOPATRA*)* I'll relay to Caesar any request you want to give me.

CLEOPATRA

> Tell him I'd like to die.

PROCULEIUS exits.

DOLABELLA

> Have you heard of me, most noble Empress?

CLEOPATRA

> I don't remember.

DOLABELLA

> I'm sure you've heard of me.

CLEOPATRA

> It doesn't matter what I've heard or known. You must be the one who laughs when boys or women tell you their dreams. Isn't that your habit?

DOLABELLA

> I don't know what you mean, madam.

CLEOPATRA

> I dreamed about an emperor called Antony. Oh, I wish I could sleep again, so I could have another dream like that!

DOLABELLA
                              If it might please ye—

CLEOPATRA
His face was as the heavens, and therein stuck
80   A sun and moon, which kept their course and lighted
The little "O," the earth.

DOLABELLA
                              Most sovereign creature—

CLEOPATRA
His legs bestrid the ocean. His reared arm
Crested the world. His voice was propertied
As all the tunèd spheres, and that to friends.
85   But when he meant to quail and shake the orb,
He was as rattling thunder. For his bounty,
There was no winter in 't, an autumn 'twas
That grew the more by reaping. His delights
Were dolphinlike; they showed his back above
90   The element they lived in. In his livery
Walked crowns and crownets. Realms and islands were
As plates dropped from his pocket.

DOLABELLA
                              Cleopatra—

CLEOPATRA
Think you there was or might be such a man
As this I dreamt of?

DOLABELLA
                              Gentle madam, no.

CLEOPATRA
95   You lie up to the hearing of the gods.
But if there be nor ever were one such,
It's past the size of dreaming. Nature wants stuff
To vie strange forms with fancy, yet t' imagine
An Antony were nature's piece 'gainst fancy,
100   Condemning shadows quite.

DOLABELLA

If you'd like—

CLEOPATRA

Authority radiated from his face, and his presence brought knowledge and order to the people of earth.

DOLABELLA

Your majesty—

CLEOPATRA

His power extended from one shore to the other, as if he straddled the ocean with his legs. When he raised his arm in command, the world trembled. He spoke exquisitely to his friends, but when he wanted to terrify the world, his voice was like thunder. There was no end to his generosity. The more he gave, the more he wanted to give. His amusements showed another side of him, one detached from his world of responsibility and duty. Kings and noblemen served him. Kingdoms and provinces dropped from his pockets like loose change.

DOLABELLA

Cleopatra—

CLEOPATRA

Do you think there ever was, or could there ever be, a man such as the one I dreamed about?

DOLABELLA

No, gentle madam.

CLEOPATRA

The gods can hear you lying! But if there ever were such a man, simple dreams could never contain his greatness. When it comes to creating fantastical things, the natural world cannot compete with imagination. And yet, if the natural world could create something like Antony, it would have a masterpiece to rival anything fantasy might construct. Antony would easily outshine all imaginary beings.

DOLABELLA
                              Hear me, good madam.
Your loss is as yourself, great, and you bear it
As answering to the weight. Would I might never
O'ertake pursued success, but I do feel,
By the rebound of yours, a grief that smites
My very heart at root.

CLEOPATRA
                              I thank you, sir.
Know you what Caesar means to do with me?

DOLABELLA
I am loath to tell you what I would you knew.

CLEOPATRA
Nay, pray you, sir.

DOLABELLA
                              Though he be honorable—

CLEOPATRA
He'll lead me, then, in triumph.

DOLABELLA
Madam, he will. I know 't.

Flourish. Enter CAESAR, PROCULEIUS, GALLUS, MAECENAS,
and other ATTENDANTS

ATTENDANTS
Make way there! Caesar!

CAESAR
Which is the Queen of Egypt?

DOLABELLA
(to CLEOPATRA*)* It is the Emperor, madam.

CLEOPATRA *kneels*

CAESAR
Arise, you shall not kneel.
I pray you, rise. Rise, Egypt.

105

110

115

DOLABELLA

Listen to me, madam. You are a remarkable person and your loss is equally remarkable. You are responding appropriately to the greatness of that loss. I hope I never achieve success if I don't feel some of your heartbroken grief right now.

CLEOPATRA

Thank you, sir. Do you know what Caesar intends to do with me?

DOLABELLA

I'm reluctant to tell you what I wish you knew.

CLEOPATRA

Please, sir—

DOLABELLA

Though he is honorable—

CLEOPATRA

He'll still parade me through Rome as a trophy of war.

DOLABELLA

I know he will, madam.

Trumpets sound a royal fanfare. CAESAR, PROCULEIUS, GALLUS, MAECENAS, *and other* ATTENDANTS *enter.*

ATTENDANTS

Stand aside for Caesar.

CAESAR

Which of these ladies is the Queen of Egypt?

DOLABELLA

(to CLEOPATRA*)* It's the Emperor, madam.

CLEOPATRA *kneels.*

CAESAR

Arise. You need not kneel to me. Please rise, Queen.

CLEOPATRA
                                  Sir, the gods
Will have it thus. My master and my lord
I must obey.

    CLEOPATRA *stands*

CAESAR
                           Take to you no hard thoughts.
The record of what injuries you did us,
Though written in our flesh, we shall remember
120   As things but done by chance.

CLEOPATRA
                              Sole sir o' th' world,
I cannot project mine own cause so well
To make it clear, but do confess I have
Been laden with like frailties which before
Have often shamed our sex.

CAESAR
                               Cleopatra, know
125   We will extenuate rather than enforce.
If you apply yourself to our intents,
Which towards you are most gentle, you shall find
A benefit in this change, but if you seek
To lay on me a cruelty by taking
130   Antony's course, you shall bereave yourself
Of my good purposes and put your children
To that destruction which I'll guard them from
If thereon you rely. I'll take my leave.

CLEOPATRA
And may, through all the world! 'Tis yours, and we,
135   Your scutcheons and your signs of conquest, shall
Hang in what place you please. Here, my good lord.

    She gives him a scroll

CLEOPATRA

> The gods have ordained it to be like this, sir. You are my lord and master. I must obey.

CLEOPATRA stands up.

CAESAR

> Don't think I blame you. Whatever injuries I received in the war, I put down to the fortunes of war.

CLEOPATRA

> You are now the sole lord of the entire world. I can't explain my cause very clearly. I must admit to having the weaknesses that all women are accused of.

CAESAR

> Cleopatra, understand that, rather than emphasize our power over you, we will soften if you accept our intentions, which are very compassionate toward you. Your acceptance will benefit you, but if you try to make me look cruel by committing suicide as Antony did, I won't be so generous.
>
> Your children will be destroyed, a fate your submission will save them from. I'll leave you now.

CLEOPATRA

> You may do whatever you want in the world. It's yours, and you may hang us, your trophies of war, anywhere you like. Here, my good lord.

She hands him a list.

CAESAR
　　You shall advise me in all for Cleopatra.

CLEOPATRA
　　This is the brief of money, plate, and jewels
　　I am possessed of. 'Tis exactly valued,
140　　Not petty things admitted. Where's Seleucus?

　　　Enter SELEUCUS

SELEUCUS
　　Here, madam.

CLEOPATRA
　　This is my treasurer. Let him speak, my lord,
　　Upon his peril, that I have reserved
　　To myself nothing.—Speak the truth, Seleucus.

SELEUCUS
145　　Madam, I had rather seal my lips
　　Than to my peril speak that which is not.

CLEOPATRA
　　What have I kept back?

SELEUCUS
　　Enough to purchase what you have made known.

CAESAR
　　Nay, blush not, Cleopatra. I approve
150　　Your wisdom in the deed.

CLEOPATRA
　　　　　　　　　　　　See, Caesar! Oh, behold
　　How pomp is followed! Mine will now be yours,
　　And, should we shift estates, yours would be mine.
　　The ingratitude of this Seleucus does
　　Even make me wild. *(to* SELEUCUS*)* O slave, of no more trust
155　　Than love that's hired!

CAESAR

You shall advise me in everything having to do with Cleopatra.

CLEOPATRA

This is the inventory of the money, silverware, dishes, and jewels that are still in my possession. It's an exact list. Not even trivial things were left out. Where's Seleucus?

SELEUCUS enters.

SELEUCUS

Here, madam.

CLEOPATRA

This is my treasurer. My lord, he will swear on his life that I haven't kept a thing.—Tell the truth, Seleucus.

SELEUCUS

Madam, I'd rather sew my lips shut than tell a lie when my life depends upon it.

CLEOPATRA

What did I keep for myself?

SELEUCUS

Enough to buy everything you have declared.

CAESAR

No, don't be ashamed, Cleopatra. You're very prudent to set a little aside.

CLEOPATRA

Look around you, Caesar. Oh, just see what happens after the pageantry is over! What is mine will be yours now. If we were to change places, what is yours would be mine. Seleucus' ingratitude makes me wild. *(to SELEUCUS)* Oh, you slave! I can't trust you any more than a prostitute.

What, goest thou back? Thou shalt
Go back, I warrant thee! But I'll catch thine eyes,
Though they had wings. Slave, soulless villain, dog!
Oh, rarely base!

CAESAR
                              Good Queen, let us entreat you—

CLEOPATRA
O Caesar, what a wounding shame is this,
160   That thou, vouchsafing here to visit me,
Doing the honor of thy lordliness
To one so meek, that mine own servant should
Parcel the sum of my disgraces by
Addition of his envy! Say, good Caesar,
165   That I some lady trifles have reserved,
Immoment toys, things of such dignity
As we greet modern friends withal, and say
Some nobler token I have kept apart
For Livia and Octavia, to induce
170   Their mediation, must I be unfolded
With one that I have bred? The gods! It smites me
Beneath the fall I have. *(to* SELEUCUS*)* Prithee, go hence,
Or I shall show the cinders of my spirit
Through th' ashes of my chance. Wert thou a man,
175   Thou wouldst have mercy on me.

CAESAR
                                        Forbear, Seleucus.
                                        Exit SELEUCUS

CLEOPATRA
Be it known that we, the greatest, are misthought
For things that others do, and when we fall
We answer others' merits in our name,
Are therefore to be pitied.

CAESAR
                              Cleopatra,
180   Not what you have reserved nor what acknowledged
Put we i' th' roll of conquest. Still be 't yours.

What are you doing? Cringing away? I'll give you a good reason to cringe, I promise you. I'll scratch out your eyes, even if they could fly. You slave! Soulless villain! Dog! Oh, that was unbelievably low!

CAESAR

Good Queen, let me implore you—

CLEOPATRA

Oh, Caesar, I am so ashamed. You condescended to visit me here, honoring my humble self with your lordly presence. And one of my own servants increases my disgrace by adding his envy! Suppose, good Caesar, that I have saved a few feminine trifles, some unimportant trinkets. These have worth only as gifts to friends. And suppose I have kept a few more expensive gifts aside for Livia and Octavia, to solicit their good wishes. Must I then be exposed by a person I've supported? By the gods! It adds another blow to the many I have already. *(to* SELEUCUS*)* Please leave, or I'll show you what's left of my spirit since my fortune was ruined. If you were a real man, you would have had mercy on me.

Livia = Octavius
Caesar's wife

CAESAR

Leave, Seleucus.

SELEUCUS *exits.*

CLEOPATRA

You should also know that as head of state, we are often blamed for the crimes of others. And though we may fall, we are still responsible for their offenses. I am therefore to be pitied.

CAESAR

Cleopatra, our conquest won't include either the things you kept back or the ones you listed. It's all still yours. Do whatever you like with it. You can trust that

Bestow it at your pleasure, and believe
Caesar's no merchant, to make prize with you
Of things that merchants sold. Therefore be cheered.
185   Make not your thoughts your prison. No, dear Queen,
For we intend so to dispose you as
Yourself shall give us counsel. Feed and sleep.
Our care and pity is so much upon you
That we remain your friend. And so, adieu.

CLEOPATRA
190   My master, and my lord!

CAESAR
       Not so. Adieu.
    Flourish. Exeunt CAESAR *and his train*

CLEOPATRA
He words me, girls, he words me, that I should not
Be noble to myself. But, hark thee, Charmian.

She whispers to CHARMIAN

IRAS
Finish, good lady. The bright day is done,
And we are for the dark.

CLEOPATRA
   (to CHARMIAN*)* Hie thee again.
195   I have spoke already, and it is provided.
Go put it to the haste.

CHARMIAN
      Madam, I will.

Enter DOLABELLA

DOLABELLA
Where's the Queen?

CHARMIAN
      Behold, sir.
            Exit

Caesar is not a merchant to haggle with you over your property. So cheer up. Don't be captured by your depressed thoughts. No, dear Queen. We want to follow your own counsel when making arrangements for you. Eat and sleep. I have so much care and pity for you that you could call me friend. And so, good-bye.

CLEOPATRA
My master and my lord!

CAESAR
Not true. Good-bye.
Trumpet flourish. CAESAR *and his entourage exit.*

CLEOPATRA
He's trying to talk me into forgetting my nobility, girls. But listen, Charmian.

She whispers to CHARMIAN.

IRAS
It's time to end it, good lady. The bright day of our lives is over, and now there will only be darkness.

CLEOPATRA
(to CHARMIAN*)* Go out again. I've already given the order, and it is ready. Hurry with your errand.

CHARMIAN
I will, madam.

DOLABELLA *enters.*

DOLABELLA
Where's the Queen?

CHARMIAN
Look, sir.

She exits.

CLEOPATRA

                    Dolabella!

DOLABELLA

Madam, as thereto sworn by your command,
Which my love makes religion to obey,
200   I tell you this: Caesar through Syria
Intends his journey, and within three days
You with your children will he send before.
Make your best use of this. I have performed
Your pleasure and my promise.

CLEOPATRA

                    Dolabella,
205   I shall remain your debtor.

DOLABELLA

                    I your servant.
Adieu, good Queen. I must attend on Caesar.

CLEOPATRA

Farewell, and thanks.

                    Exit DOLABELLA
                    Now, Iras, what think'st thou?
Thou an Egyptian puppet shalt be shown
In Rome, as well as I. Mechanic slaves
210   With greasy aprons, rules, and hammers shall
Uplift us to the view. In their thick breaths,
Rank of gross diet, shall be enclouded,
And forced to drink their vapor.

IRAS

                    The gods forbid!

CLEOPATRA

Nay, 'tis most certain, Iras. Saucy lictors
215   Will catch at us like strumpets, and scald rhymers
Ballad us out o' tune. The quick comedians
Extemporally will stage us and present
Our Alexandrian revels. Antony
Shall be brought drunken forth, and I shall see

CLEOPATRA

Dolabella.

DOLABELLA

Madam, according to my promise—which my love to you has made a religious vow—I tell you that Caesar intends to travel through Syria. Within three days you and your children will be sent ahead. Make the best use of this information you can. I have done your bidding and fulfilled my promise.

CLEOPATRA

Dolabella, I will always be in debt to you.

DOLABELLA

And I your servant. Good-bye, good Queen. I must go attend Caesar.

CLEOPATRA

Farewell, and thanks.

DOLABELLA exits.

Now, Iras, what do you think? You will be exhibited in Rome along with me, like Egyptian puppets. Crude slaves with greasy aprons, rulers, and hammers shall lift us up so everyone can see. Their stinking breath will form a cloud around us, and we'll be forced to inhale it.

IRAS

The gods forbid!

CLEOPATRA

lictors = Roman officers who assisted the judge

No, it's certain, Iras. Insolent lictors will paw us as if we were streetwalkers. Disreputable minstrels will write bawdy songs about us. Hotheaded comedians will stage impromptu impersonations of us and depict the celebrations we had in Alexandria. Antony will be portrayed as a drunk, and I'll see some boy with a squeaking voice play Cleopatra as if I were a whore.

220 Some squeaking Cleopatra boy my greatness
I' th' posture of a whore.

IRAS
                                    Oh, the good gods!

CLEOPATRA
Nay, that's certain.

IRAS
I'll never see 't! For I am sure mine nails
Are stronger than mine eyes.

CLEOPATRA
                                    Why, that's the way
225 To fool their preparation and to conquer
Their most absurd intents.

Enter CHARMIAN

                                    Now, Charmian!
Show me, my women, like a queen. Go fetch
My best attires. I am again for Cydnus,
To meet Mark Antony.—Sirrah Iras, go.—
230 Now, noble Charmian, we'll dispatch indeed,
And when thou hast done this chare I'll give thee leave
To play till doomsday. *(to* IRAS*)* Bring our crown and all.
                          Exit IRAS. *A noise within*
Wherefore's this noise?

Enter a GUARDSMAN

GUARDSMAN
                                    Here is a rural fellow
That will not be denied your Highness' presence.
235 He brings you figs.

CLEOPATRA
Let him come in.
                                    Exit GUARDSMAN

IRAS

Oh, the good gods!

CLEOPATRA

No, that's the truth.

IRAS

I'll never see it. I know my nails are stronger than my eyes; I'll scratch them out.

CLEOPATRA

Why, that's just the way to frustrate their plans and defeat their absurd intentions.

CHARMIAN *enters.*

Now, Charmian! Women, dress me like a queen. Go get my best clothes. I will once again be as fine as when I went to Cydnus to meet Marc Antony.—Iras, go.— Now, Charmian, we'll be quick indeed. And after you've done this chore, I'll give you permission to amuse yourself until doomsday. *(to* IRAS*)* Bring our crown and all the royal symbols of office.

IRAS *exits. A noise offstage.*

What's that noise?

A GUARDSMAN *enters.*

GUARDSMAN

There's a farmer here who won't leave without seeing your Highness. He has brought you figs.

CLEOPATRA

Let him come in.

The GUARDSMAN *exits.*

What poor an instrument
May do a noble deed! He brings me liberty.
My resolution's placed, and I have nothing
Of woman in me. Now from head to foot
240   I am marble-constant. Now the fleeting moon
No planet is of mine.

Enter GUARDSMAN, *and* COUNTRYMAN *bringing in a basket*

GUARDSMAN

                   This is the man.

CLEOPATRA
Avoid, and leave him.

                         Exit GUARDSMAN

Hast thou the pretty worm of Nilus there,
That kills and pains not?

COUNTRYMAN
245   Truly, I have him, but I would not be the party that should
desire you to touch him, for his biting is immortal. Those
that do die of it do seldom or never recover.

CLEOPATRA
Remember'st thou any that have died on 't?

COUNTRYMAN
Very many, men and women too. I heard of one of them no
250   longer than yesterday—a very honest woman, but
something given to lie, as a woman should not do but in the
way of honesty—how she died of the biting of it, what pain
she felt. Truly, she makes a very good report o' th' worm.
But he that will believe all that they say shall never be saved
255   by half that they do. But this is most falliable, the worm's an
odd worm.

CLEOPATRA
Get thee hence, farewell.

What a poor instrument, that can do such a noble deed! He brings me freedom. My mind is made up. There's nothing of the weak woman left in me. Now from head to foot I'm as firm as marble. Now the inconstant moon has nothing to do with me.

The GUARDSMAN *enters with a* COUNTRYMAN, *who carries a basket.*

GUARDSMAN
This is the man.

CLEOPATRA
Leave us.

The GUARDSMAN *exits.*

Do you have in there the pretty snake of the Nile that kills without pain?

COUNTRYMAN
I certainly do have him, but I wouldn't advise you to touch him. His bite is fatal. People who die of it seldom or never recover.

CLEOPATRA
Do you remember anyone who died of it?

COUNTRYMAN
Many people, men and women alike. I heard of one just yesterday. She was a very honest woman but rather inclined to lie—which a woman shouldn't do unless she's protecting her reputation. I heard how she died of its bite, how much pain she felt. Indeed, she gives a very good testimony of the snake's power. But if you believe everything they say, you won't be saved by half of what they do. But this is a sure thing: the snake's an odd snake.

CLEOPATRA
You may leave now. Farewell.

COUNTRYMAN
I wish you all joy of the worm.

He sets down his basket

CLEOPATRA
Farewell.

COUNTRYMAN
260   You must think this, look you, that the worm will do his
kind.

CLEOPATRA
Ay, ay. Farewell.

COUNTRYMAN
Look you, the worm is not to be trusted but in the keeping
of wise people, for indeed there is no goodness in the worm.

CLEOPATRA
265   Take thou no care. It shall be heeded.

COUNTRYMAN
Very good. Give it nothing, I pray you, for it is not worth the
feeding.

CLEOPATRA
Will it eat me?

COUNTRYMAN
You must not think I am so simple but I know the devil
270   himself will not eat a woman. I know that a woman is a dish
for the gods, if the devil dress her not. But, truly, these same
whoreson devils do the gods great harm in their women, for
in every ten that they make, the devils mar five.

CLEOPATRA
Well, get thee gone. Farewell.

COUNTRYMAN
275   Yes, forsooth. I wish you joy o' th' worm.

Exit

COUNTRYMAN
I hope you are pleased with the snake.

He sets down the basket.

CLEOPATRA
Farewell.

COUNTRYMAN
You must know that the snake will act according to his nature.

CLEOPATRA
Yes, yes. Farewell.

COUNTRYMAN
Listen, the snake is dangerous unless handled by people who are used to him. There isn't any kindness in the snake.

CLEOPATRA
Don't worry; we'll remember your warnings.

COUNTRYMAN
Good. Don't feed it, I beg you. It's not worth feeding.

CLEOPATRA
Will it eat me?

COUNTRYMAN
Don't think I'm so dumb that I don't know that the devil himself won't eat a woman. I know that a woman is a dish fit only for the gods, as long as the devil hasn't prepared the meal. But devils cause a lot of trouble for the gods regarding their women. For every ten women the gods make, the devils ruin five.

CLEOPATRA
Well, you can go now. Farewell.

COUNTRYMAN
Yes, truly, I wish you good luck with the snake.

He exits.

Enter IRAS *with royal attire*

CLEOPATRA
    Give me my robe. Put on my crown. I have
    Immortal longings in me. Now no more
    The juice of Egypt's grape shall moist this lip.

The women dress her

    Yare, yare, good Iras, quick. Methinks I hear
280   Antony call. I see him rouse himself
    To praise my noble act. I hear him mock
    The luck of Caesar, which the gods give men
    To excuse their after wrath.—Husband, I come!
    Now to that name my courage prove my title!
285   I am fire and air, my other elements
    I give to baser life.—So, have you done?
    Come then and take the last warmth of my lips.
    Farewell, kind Charmian. Iras, long farewell.

She kisses them. IRAS *falls and dies*

    Have I the aspic in my lips? Dost fall?
290   If thou and nature can so gently part,
    The stroke of death is as a lover's pinch,
    Which hurts, and is desired. Dost thou lie still?
    If thus thou vanishest, thou tell'st the world
    It is not worth leave-taking.

CHARMIAN
295   Dissolve, thick cloud, and rain, that I may say
    The gods themselves do weep!

CLEOPATRA
                          This proves me base.
    If she first meet the curlèd Antony,

IRAS *enters, carrying* CLEOPATRA*'s royal regalia.*

CLEOPATRA

Give me my robe. Put on my crown. I long to be immortal. I won't drink Egyptian wine again.

CHARMIAN *and* IRAS *begin to dress her.*

Quickly, quickly, good Iras, quickly. I think I hear Antony call me. I see him revive himself to praise my noble act. I hear him mock Caesar's luck, which the gods give to men in order to balance out their subsequent wrath. Husband, I'm coming! Now let my courage prove my title as wife. I am now made of fire and air, and I leave the other elements, earth and water, to this mortal life. So, are you done? Come then, kiss me and take the last bit of warmth from my lips. Good-bye, kind Charmian. Iras, I won't see you again for a long time.

She kisses them. IRAS *collapses and dies.*

Do I have the asp's poison on my lips? Did you fall? If you can leave your body so easily, then the touch of death is like a lover's pinch, which hurts but is desired. Do you lie still? If you leave like that, you tell the world that it's not worthy of a good-bye.

CHARMIAN

Clouds, dissolve into rain, so that I could say the gods themselves are weeping!

CLEOPATRA

This proves that I'm petty: if Iras meets Antony before me, he'll want her first and give her the kiss that is my bliss to have.

He'll make demand of her and spend that kiss
Which is my heaven to have. —Come, thou mortal wretch,

She places an asp on her breast

300   With thy sharp teeth this knot intrinsicate
Of life at once untie. Poor venomous fool
Be angry and dispatch. Oh, couldst thou speak,
That I might hear thee call great Caesar ass
Unpolicied!

CHARMIAN
                     O eastern star!

CLEOPATRA
                              Peace, peace!
305   Dost thou not see my baby at my breast,
That sucks the nurse asleep?

CHARMIAN
                              Oh, break! Oh, break!

CLEOPATRA
As sweet as balm, as soft as air, as gentle—
O Antony!—Nay, I will take thee too.

Applying another asp to her arm

What should I stay—

Dies

CHARMIAN
310   In this wild world? So, fare thee well.
Now boast thee, Death, in thy possession lies
A lass unparalleled. Downy windows, close,

She closes CLEOPATRA*'s eyes*

Come, you deadly villain.

She puts the snake on her breast.

Separate me from life with your sharp teeth. Poor poisonous fool, be angry and bite. Oh, if you could speak, I might hear you call Caesar an ass who's been outsmarted!

CHARMIAN

Oh, eastern star!

CLEOPATRA

Quiet, quiet! Don't you see my baby suckling at my breast so that its nurse will fall asleep?

CHARMIAN

Oh, if my heart would only break!

CLEOPATRA

The poison is as sweet as balm, as soft as air, as gentle—Oh, Antony!—No, I'll take you too.

She puts another snake on her arm.

Why should I stay—

She dies.

CHARMIAN

In this vile world? So, good-bye. Now, Death, you can boast that you have an incomparable girl in your possession. Close, soft eyes.

She closes CLEOPATRA's *eyes.*

And golden Phoebus never be beheld
Of eyes again so royal! Your crown's awry.
315   I'll mend it and then play—

Enter the GUARD, *rustling in*

FIRST GUARD
Where's the Queen?

CHARMIAN
                              Speak softly. Wake her not.

FIRST GUARD
Caesar hath sent—

CHARMIAN
                              Too slow a messenger.

She applies an asp to herself.

Oh, come apace, dispatch! I partly feel thee.

FIRST GUARD
(calling) Approach, ho! All's not well. Caesar's beguiled.

SECOND GUARD
320   There's Dolabella sent from Caesar. Call him.

                              Exit SECOND GUARD

FIRST GUARD
What work is here, Charmian? Is this well done?

CHARMIAN
It is well done and fitting for a princess
Descended of so many royal kings.
Ah, soldier!

CHARMIAN *dies*

Enter DOLABELLA

The sun will never be seen by such royal eyes again. Your crown is crooked. I'll straighten it, then play—

The GUARDS *rush in noisily.*

FIRST GUARD

Where's the Queen?

CHARMIAN

Speak softly. Don't wake her.

FIRST GUARD

Caesar has sent—

CHARMIAN

Too slow a messenger.

She applies an asp to herself.

Oh, come quickly! I almost feel you.

FIRST GUARD

(calling) Come in. Ho! All's not well. Caesar's been deceived.

SECOND GUARD

There's Dolabella, who was sent from Caesar. Call him.

The SECOND GUARD *exits.*

FIRST GUARD

What kind of work is this, Charmian? Is this well done?

CHARMIAN

It is well done, and appropriate for a princess who has descended from so many royal kings. Ah, soldier!

She dies.

DOLABELLA *enters.*

DOLABELLA
325   How goes it here?

SECOND GUARD
                    All dead.

DOLABELLA
                            Caesar, thy thoughts
Touch their effects in this. Thyself art coming
To see performed the dreaded act which thou
So sought'st to hinder.

Enter CAESAR *and all his train, marching*

ALL
    A way there, a way for Caesar!

DOLABELLA
330   O sir, you are too sure an augurer.
That you did fear is done.

CAESAR
    Bravest at the last,
She leveled at our purposes and, being royal,
Took her own way. The manner of their deaths?
335   I do not see them bleed.

DOLABELLA
                  Who was last with them?

FIRST GUARD
    A simple countryman that brought her figs.
This was his basket.

CAESAR
               Poisoned, then.

FIRST GUARD
                      Oh, Caesar,
This Charmian lived but now. She stood and spake.
I found her trimming up the diadem
340   On her dead mistress. Tremblingly she stood
And on the sudden dropped.

DOLABELLA

What's going on in here?

SECOND GUARD

They're all dead.

DOLABELLA

Caesar, you thought this would happen. You're coming here yourself to see the dreaded act you had tried to stop.

CAESAR and his entourage enter, marching.

ALL

Step aside, step aside for Caesar!

DOLABELLA

Oh, sir, you are too good at predicting the future. What you were afraid of has happened.

CAESAR

She was bravest at the end. She knew what I intended to do with her and, being royal, she took her own way out. How did they die? I don't see any blood.

DOLABELLA

Who was with them last?

FIRST GUARD

A simple country farmer who brought her figs. This was the basket.

CAESAR

They were poisoned, then.

FIRST GUARD

Oh, Caesar, this Charmian lived until a moment ago. She stood and spoke. I found her adjusting the crown on her dead mistress. She stood trembling, then suddenly dropped dead.

CAESAR
                              Oh, noble weakness!
If they had swallowed poison, 'twould appear
By external swelling, but she looks like sleep,
As she would catch another Antony
345 In her strong toil of grace.

DOLABELLA
                              Here on her breast
There is a vent of blood, and something blown.
The like is on her arm.

FIRST GUARD
This is an aspic's trail, and these fig leaves
Have slime upon them, such as th' aspic leaves
350 Upon the caves of Nile.

CAESAR
                              Most probable
That so she died, for her physician tells me
She hath pursued conclusions infinite
Of easy ways to die. Take up her bed
And bear her women from the monument.
355 She shall be buried by her Antony.
No grave upon the earth shall clip in it
A pair so famous. High events as these
Strike those that make them, and their story is
No less in pity than his glory which
360 Brought them to be lamented. Our army shall
In solemn show attend this funeral,
And then to Rome. Come, Dolabella, see
High order in this great solemnity.
                              Exeunt, bearing the dead bodies

CAESAR

> Oh, noble weakness! If they had swallowed poison, it would be evident by external swelling. But she looks like she's asleep, as if she would charm another Antony.

DOLABELLA

> Here on her breast there's a little bloody mark. There's a similar mark on her arm.

FIRST GUARD

> This is an asp's trail, and these fig leaves have slime on them, just like the kind that asps deposit on the caves by the Nile.

CAESAR

> That's probably how she died. Her doctor told me she had searched for an infinite number of easy ways to die. Pick up her bed and carry her ladies out of the tomb. She shall be buried next to her Antony. No other grave on earth shall hold a pair this famous. Momentous events like these strike those that cause them. Antony and Cleopatra's story is as pitiable as my military exploits are glorious. Our army shall somberly attend this funeral and then depart for Rome. Come, Dolabella. See that there is a dignified splendor to this great solemnity.

> *They exit, with the* GUARDS *carrying* CLEOPATRA'*s bed and the two ladies.*

Notes